COLD★WAR
OKLAHOMA

COLD ★ WAR
OKLAHOMA

L ANDRY B REWER

FOREWORD BY BOB BURKE

THE
History
PRESS

Published by The History Press
Charleston, SC
www.historypress.com

Copyright © 2019 by Landry Brewer
All rights reserved

First published 2019

Manufactured in the United States

ISBN 9781467142250

Library of Congress Control Number: 2018966330

For Erin, Dylan, Kelsey, MacKinley, Quinn and Spence.

CONTENTS

FOREWORD

For the past three decades, Americans have been spared the constant fear of nuclear war. However, for generations living during the Cold War, from about 1947 to 1991, the fear of World War III and atomic warheads was real. American officials encouraged the development of atomic weapons that ended World War II. The Soviet Union followed suit, and the arms race began.

The day the world perhaps came closest to the Cold War becoming a nuclear war was October 24, 1962, during the Cuban missile crisis. It was a dangerous and direct confrontation between the United States and the Soviet Union when the U.S. learned Soviets were building missile sites in Cuba, just ninety miles from Florida. President John F. Kennedy harshly threatened the Soviets and demanded the construction stop. The Soviets called an American blockade around Cuba an act of aggression.

On October 24, American reconnaissance flights showed construction of the missile sites was continuing and Soviet ships were sailing to Cuba. President Kennedy told his advisors that it appeared only a U.S. attack on Cuba would remove the missiles. American military forces were raised to DEFCON 2, meaning war involving the Strategic Air Command was imminent. A diplomatic solution was reached, but it was a day when nuclear war between the world's two superpowers was just one button and one command away for those hovering over control panels at missile sites, including silos built at a dozen sites near Altus Air Force Base, such as those in the southwest Oklahoma locations of Willow, Cache, Granite and Hobart.

In this book, Professor Landry Brewer expertly chronicles Oklahoma's role during the Cold War. With first-person information gleaned during interviews with people ranging from missile technicians to civil defense officials, he paints a comprehensive story of how the Cold War affected the daily lives of Oklahomans, particularly in the 1950s and 1960s, when Soviet aggression rose in intensity and little was done to stop the proliferation of nuclear weapons and missile systems. There is even the little-known tale of a Soviet spy who was educated at the University of Oklahoma and joined the faculty in Norman.

In addition to the exciting story of constructing and arming missile silos in Oklahoma, Professor Brewer superbly writes of local cities and towns forming civil defense departments. Sirens, normally used to warn Oklahomans of approaching severe weather, were tested during mock drills. Families and towns stocked their bomb shelters with food and water. Families enrolled in radioactive monitoring classes. In each Oklahoma high school classroom, a Geiger counter became a standard teaching tool.

I am unaware of anyone, before the publication of this book, researching and telling this important Oklahoma story. Professor Brewer proves the theory that Oklahoma's incredible heritage is not about places and events, it is about our people—men and women who played necessary roles in Oklahoma during the Cold War.

—Bob Burke

Oklahoma attorney, author and historian Bob Burke has written more historical nonfiction books (130) than anyone in history.

ACKNOWLEDGEMENTS

I am indebted to several people who assisted in bringing this book to life, starting with my patient editor at The History Press, Ben Gibson. He never showed the strain that must have resulted from my frequent emails.

Mike Clark and his family; the administrator of www.atlasmissilesilo.com; and the Granite, Oklahoma school system allowed me to walk the grounds of former Atlas missile sites and learn more than I would have had I not experienced them firsthand. Their help made the sites concrete for me, and I hope that I have, in turn, made them concrete for readers.

Rotary Clubs and Kiwanis Clubs from Shamrock, Texas, to Weatherford, Oklahoma, as well as the Stafford Air & Space Museum in Weatherford; Southwestern Oklahoma State University (SWOSU) in Weatherford and Sayre; and the Kiowa County Historical Society provided attentive audiences during my presentations about Cold War matters that include material appearing in this book.

Jerry Brewer, Basil Weatherly and Billy Word gave of their time, patiently answered my questions and shared Cold War memories and mementos. Their contributions were immense, and this book would lack greatly without them.

Fellow Okie and Columbia College history professor Brad Lookingbill has enthusiastically encouraged my research and writing about this aspect of state history, for which I am grateful.

Elizabeth Bass of the Oklahoma Historical Society provided valuable editorial input and other help along the way.

Holley Brewer overcame her historic dislike of history and generously provided her own editorial suggestions that improved the manuscript.

Bob Burke graciously read manuscript portions and provided much-appreciated encouragement.

A good friend who has professional experience combatting foreign espionage inside the United States was extremely helpful in this process; he not only enthusiastically supported this project, but he also posed probing questions that made me think more thoroughly about how spies ply their trade as I researched and wrote about Maurice Halperin.

DeAun Ivester and the staff of the Elk City Carnegie Library helped me search the library's archives, which contributed significantly to this book.

Phillip Fitzsimmons, digitization librarian at the Al Harris Library on the Southwestern Oklahoma State University campus in Weatherford, spent much time and expended much energy combing the library's archives, providing me with invaluable resources, information and photographs. His efforts have improved this book mightily.

Thank you to the SWOSU administration, especially President Randy Beutler, Provost James South, Sayre campus dean Sherron Manning, dean of arts and sciences Peter Grant and Department of Social Sciences chair John Hayden, for your support, encouragement and motivation.

Additionally, thank you to my SWOSU colleagues at the Sayre campus and those in the Department of Social Sciences. I'm proud to serve with you.

Each in his own way, Kevin, ReDon and Travis Brewer helped shape me into the person I am today. Thank you.

Acknowledgements wouldn't be complete without thanking my mother, Sherlene Brewer. Thanks for everything, Mom.

My twin brother and fellow talk radio show host, Nathan, is the writer, speaker and thinker I aspire to be. Bouncing ideas off of him and discussing the book's content was of great benefit. His friendship, support and love are of even greater benefit.

And finally, to my wife, Erin, and to my kids, thank you for enduring what must have seemed over the last two and a half years like nonstop talk of missiles, spies and fallout shelters. Without you, this book wouldn't be possible, because your love and support mean everything.

INTRODUCTION

The Cold War was frightening. For decades, Americans feared that civilization would be gone with the wind of a nuclear cataclysm if the Cold War between the United States and the Soviet Union got hot. Intimately acquainted with the destructive capabilities of wind, Oklahomans felt the fear.

Lulled by the sense of complacency that follows victory, postwar Americans wanted a return to normalcy after World War II ended. But the United States, long a country that valued the safety and security of two friendly neighbors to the north and south and two oceans to the east and west providing a buffer between it and any would-be adversaries, found itself in a new role—leader of the free world. On the other side of this bipolar struggle was the Soviet Union, the original "Red Menace" that had enslaved first its own people under Communist rule and then millions more in Eastern Europe as it spread its influence and forced Communism on those people the Nazis had conquered just a few years earlier.

Believing that Joseph Stalin had replaced Adolf Hitler as the mustachioed madman bent on the domination of Europe and the world, and with the British and other Western Europeans lacking the means and opportunity to stop the Soviet leader, the United States stepped in. As the only nation in the world economically and militarily capable of stopping the Soviet Union from expanding its territory and influence, American foreign policy in the late 1940s became increasingly interventionist.

President Truman put the Congress, the nation and the world on notice: the United States would stop Communism's attempt to subvert the will of sovereign peoples with its money, its influence and, if necessary, with its weapons, including the atomic bomb.

As the nation readied itself for what President Kennedy would call a "long twilight struggle," Oklahomans did their part. From all over the state, Oklahomans joined the nationwide effort to support American democracy and oppose Communism at a time when it appeared that the Soviet Union was intent on ending self-government and individual freedom among our European allies. With the acquisition of atomic and thermonuclear weapons, it seemed intent on doing the same—or worse—to the United States.

Oklahoma's civilians, politicians and military personnel answered the call. Military bases in the state were reopened and expanded. Long-range missiles that were part of the nation's offensive nuclear arsenal were operated. Civilians prepared to survive the effects of a nuclear attack. State and national politicians from Oklahoma readied their governments to protect the people they served and preserve a way of life in the face of grave international danger.

The reality of danger becomes more abstract with the passing of time. The Cold War was dangerous for the world, for the nation and for Oklahoma. We need to understand how dangerous. We need to remember. This book tells an important story. It reminds us how dangerous the world was for

Oklahoma map locating ten of the cities featured prominently in the state's Cold War activities. *Courtesy of Southwestern Oklahoma State University graphic designer Kyle Wright.*

forty-five years when atomic weapons became thermonuclear weapons; how increasingly destructive those weapons became; and how close the United States and the Soviet Union came to using them against each other. It also reminds us of Oklahoma's role.

In 1961, the Cold War hadn't reached its midpoint. In a speech to the United Nations that year, President Kennedy said, "Every man, woman and child lives under a nuclear sword of Damocles, hanging by the slenderest of threads, capable of being cut at any moment by accident or miscalculation or by madness."[1]

That danger was as real for Oklahoma as it was for the rest of the nation—in some ways more so. From Enid to McAlester, from Tulsa to Altus, from Elk City to Oklahoma City, Oklahomans did their part to keep themselves, their families and their fellow citizens safe. From building missile sites to digging fallout shelters, and from serving in the military to serving in the government, Oklahomans fought that long twilight struggle when the fate of the world hung in the air.

Oklahomans—with the exception of one proven traitor in their midst—showed themselves worthy of this righteous cause.

And this is worthy of remembering.

1

COLD WAR ORIGINS

Though the United States and the Soviet Union were allies during World War II, the two nations became adversaries when the war ended in 1945. The Nazi military had taken control of Eastern Europe by the end of 1941. When the war ended four years later, the Red Army, having defeated the German army on its march to Berlin, controlled that territory for the Soviet Union. "The Soviet Union occupied East Europe. This crucial result of World War II destroyed the Grand Alliance and gave birth to the Cold War," according to historians Stephen Ambrose and Douglas Brinkley.[2]

At the February 1945 Yalta Conference, three months before World War II ended in Europe with Germany's surrender, leaders of the United States, Great Britain and the Soviet Union—Franklin Roosevelt, Winston Churchill and Joseph Stalin, respectively—agreed to postwar arrangements in Europe. In return for the Soviet Union joining the war against Japan within three months of Germany's surrender, Roosevelt and Churchill consented to allow the Soviet Union to exert control over Eastern Europe—but only if Stalin promised to allow free elections there. Stalin agreed. However, Stalin "never accepted the Western interpretation of the Yalta agreements." The Soviet Union controlled Eastern Europe and did not intend to relinquish that control.[3]

The United States dropped two atomic bombs on the Japanese cities Hiroshima and Nagasaki in August 1945. Shortly thereafter, the Japanese government surrendered and World War II ended. As conditions between the former war allies worsened and the Soviet Union consolidated control over much of Europe, former British prime minister Churchill played the role of prophet when he delivered a March 5, 1946 speech in President Truman's home state at Westminster College in Fulton, Missouri, with the president seated nearby. In what is now known as the "Iron Curtain" speech, Churchill said this about Soviet control of the eastern portion of a divided Europe:

> *From Stettin in the Baltic to Trieste in the Adriatic an "iron curtain" has descended across the continent. Behind that line lie all the capitals of the ancient states of Central and Eastern Europe. Warsaw, Berlin, Prague, Vienna, Budapest, Belgrade, Bucharest and Sofia; all these famous cities and the populations around them lie in what I must call the Soviet sphere, and all are subject, in one form or another, not only to Soviet influence but to a very high and in some cases increasing measure of control from Moscow.*[4]

By 1947, President Truman was intensifying his foreign policy against the Soviet Union and Communism. State Department official William C. Bullitt gave a mid-1947 speech at the National War College in which he likened Stalin to Hitler and said that the Soviet Union wanted to conquer the world. Communists threatened to replace the British-supported Greek government, though British aid and forty thousand British troops in Greece were preventing that from happening. When the British government informed the Americans in February 1947 that no further aid would be forthcoming and British troops would soon return home, President Truman decided that the United States must intervene. Truman believed that if Greece fell to Communism, its neighbor Turkey, which had been pressured by the Soviet Union to allow it a military presence there, would be next to fall. On March 12, 1947, President Truman addressed a joint session of Congress, appealing for American aid for both countries and announcing the Truman Doctrine: "I believe that it must be the policy of the United States to support free peoples who are resisting attempted subjugation by armed minorities or by outside pressures."[5]

Congress granted Truman's request of $400 million in aid for Greece and Turkey, and the United States began a new era. "For the first time in its history, the United States had chosen to intervene during a period of general peace in the affairs of peoples outside North and South America." President Truman articulated the American government's new policy of containment, through which the nation sought to stop the spread of Soviet Communism.[6]

According to Truman biographer David McCullough, American policy toward the Soviet Union changed markedly after Secretary of State George Marshall returned from a 1947 meeting with his European counterparts. Marshall told Truman that the United States could not deal with the Soviets, and diplomacy was destined to fail. By late 1947, the conflict between the United States and the Soviet Union was being called the "Cold War" by columnist Walter Lippmann. Though the expression had been used earlier, Lippmann was the first to attach it to the increasingly hostile East-West divide.[7]

Secretary Marshall returned to Washington on Saturday, April 26, 1947, shocked by what he had seen in Berlin and Western Europe during his trip, which included a visit to Moscow for talks with the Soviet government. Slow to recover economically from the ravages of World War II, Western Europe was teetering on the brink of economic collapse and needed to be rescued. Marshall instructed his State Department to formulate a plan to give economic aid that would help revive Europe's economy. "Millions of people were slowly starving. A collapse in Europe would mean revolution and a tailspin for the American economy."[8] Marshall announced what came to be called the Marshall Plan—officially the European Recovery Program—to help prevent economic collapse and starvation, ensure that the United States had economically viable trading partners in Europe and stave off a Communist takeover of Western Europe in a June 5 speech at Harvard:

> *Our policy is directed not against any country or doctrine, but against hunger, poverty, desperation and chaos. Its purpose should be the revival of a working economy in the world so as to permit the emergence of political and social conditions in which free institutions can exist.*[9]

The amount requested for Marshall Plan aid to Europe was $17 billion, and fearing Congress would refuse to appropriate the money, President Truman met with Speaker of the House Sam Rayburn to sell the idea. According to McCullough, "Truman said there was no way of telling how many hundreds of thousands of people would starve to death in Europe and that this must not happen, not if it could be prevented." Truman "was also sure…that if Europe went 'down the drain' in a depression, the United States would follow." He said to the speaker that they had "both lived through one depression, and we don't want to have to live through another one, do we, Sam?" Congress passed the Marshall Plan in April 1948, almost one year after Marshall's Harvard speech.[10]

Also important for American Cold War military operations and foreign policy was passage by Congress of the National Security Act of 1947. In February, President Truman sent the bill to Congress to reorganize the nation's military so that its several branches were all brought under the oversight "of a single Department of Defense and a single Secretary of Defense." In addition to the Department of Defense, the legislation also created a separate air force, removing it from the army. Additionally, the act created the National Security Council and the Central Intelligence Agency.[11]

Since World War II ended, the eastern portion of Berlin had been occupied by the Soviets, with the Americans, British and French in the western portion of the city, each country within its own sector. In the summer of 1948, Joseph Stalin ordered a blockade of Berlin to prevent the Western powers from gaining access to the city by ground or water transport in an attempt to starve the city into submission and force the democracies out of their sectors. Opinions within the American government differed as to what the country's response should be, though President Truman was adamant that the United States stand its ground. Army chief of staff Omar Bradley recommended to President Truman that access to West Berlin could be gained by air. Soon, "air transport…flying round-the-clock missions into Berlin, supplying up to 13,000 tons of goods per day" commenced, and "[t]he Berlin airlift caught the imagination of the world."[12] With the airlift lasting just under one year before Stalin finally called the blockade off in 1949,

> *official U.S. Air Force numbers include: total cargo delivered to Berlin—2,325,809 tons, 1,783,573 of those by the Air Force and 542,236 tons by the Royal Air Forces of Britain, Australia and New Zealand, along with private aircraft chartered by the British government. The total number of flights into Berlin was recorded as 277,569— 189,963 by the Americans, and 87,606 by the British and their Commonwealth partners.*[13]

The triumph of the Berlin Airlift overlapped with another diplomatic triumph: the North Atlantic Treaty Organization (NATO). Delivering his inaugural address after winning the 1948 presidential election, Truman "pledged…to aid those European nations willing to defend themselves." Carrying out the president's wishes, Secretary of State Dean Acheson brokered the North Atlantic Treaty, which was signed on April 4, 1949, in Washington, D.C. "Britain, France, Belgium, the Netherlands, Italy, Portugal, Denmark, Iceland, Norway, Canada, and the United States pledged themselves to mutual assistance in case of aggression against any of the signatories."[14] NATO was born, furthering the cause of containment in Europe.

Any feelings of triumph were overwhelmed by concern as summer became fall in 1949. In early September, an air force plane discovered radioactivity over the northern Pacific Ocean. On Monday, September 19, the scientists who reviewed the radioactive samples concluded that the Soviet Union had, for the first time, detonated an atomic bomb. The American atomic monopoly had ended. President Truman was informed the next day. He released a statement to the press on Friday, September 23, informing the American public, "[a]nd though there was no panic in the country, the fears and tensions of the Cold War were greatly amplified. It was a different world now."[15]

Early the next month, the years-long Chinese civil war, fought between Communists led by Mao Tse-tung and Nationalists led by American ally Chiang Kai-shek, came to an end. Although the United States had spent billions of dollars supporting Chiang in hopes of staving off Communism's advances in China since World War II ended, it was not enough. Just one week after President Truman informed the American people that the Soviet Union had acquired its own atomic bomb, "the People's Republic of China, the most numerous Communist nation in the world, with more than 500 million people, one fifth of humanity, was officially inaugurated."[16]

That same month, October 1949, the Cold War intensified yet again. Soon after President Truman informed the nation that the Soviets had the atomic bomb, American officials began to discuss pursuing "a thermonuclear or hydrogen weapon—a superbomb, or 'Super'—which would have more than ten times the destructive power of the bombs dropped on Hiroshima and Nagasaki." The belief was that if the Soviets had the capacity to build an atomic bomb, they would likely have the means and desire to create their own thermonuclear bomb, which meant that the United States must also have this weapon. President Truman agreed with his advisors, and on January 31, 1950, he officially signed off on developing the hydrogen—or thermonuclear—bomb.[17]

Because of Communist ascendancy in China, the Soviet acquisition of the atomic bomb, and the specter of a Soviet thermonuclear bomb—and the domestic political pressure that these events created—on January 30, 1950, President Truman tasked the Department of State and the Department of Defense with reviewing the nation's defense and foreign policy. A report was prepared, forwarded to the National Security Council, and then delivered to the president as National Security Council Paper #68, or simply NSC 68. The report advocated a massive military buildup in an effort to offset Communist gains and discourage further Soviet expansion. It predicted that "the Soviets would probably achieve nuclear equality by 1954," and although "no cost estimates were included, the figures discussed with Truman ranged from $40 to $50 billion a year, at least three times the current military budget." The report ended ominously by telling President Truman, "The whole success hangs ultimately on recognition by this government, the American people and all the peoples that the Cold War is in fact a real war in which the survival of the world is at stake."[18]

That summer, Communist North Korean troops invaded South Korea. The United States would fight a three-year war trying to restore the status quo ante bellum and prevent a Communist takeover of the southern half of the Korean peninsula. Then, in the 1960s, Americans began fighting another war, itself a decade-long conflict in Southeast Asia to prevent a Communist takeover in South Vietnam. Between the two Cold War–inspired hot conflicts, the United States and the Soviet Union would reach the brink of nuclear war, each with long-range bombers and ballistic missiles that could fly thousands of miles and deliver nuclear bombs capable of inflicting civilization-ending destruction. Then, as the 1970s became the 1980s, the nuclear arms race between the United States and the Soviet Union resumed, and fears of nuclear war reemerged. Throughout these decades, Americans—including Oklahomans—hoped for the best but prepared for the worst. The Cold War ushered in a different world indeed.

2

THE MISSILES OF OKLAHOMA

To counter the Soviet Union's Cold War nuclear threat, the U.S. government began creating an offensive nuclear capability in the 1950s that included intercontinental ballistic missiles (ICBMs) capable of reaching the Soviet Union. The first American ICBM was the Atlas missile. Southwest Oklahoma near Altus Air Force Base played a crucial role in the nation's nuclear arsenal from 1960 through 1965 by building several missile launch sites that housed Atlas F missiles. The state was rewarded with jobs, massive amounts of dollars spent here and the satisfaction of deterring Soviet aggression while defending the nation against possible attack.

The Soviet Union's successful August 1957 ICBM launch, followed by its October 1957 launch of Sputnik, created the illusion of a missile gap. Many believed that the Soviets were ahead of U.S. nuclear weapons development, tipping the Cold War power balance in the Soviets' favor. Some even feared the Soviets would launch a nuclear first strike, destroy American Strategic Air Command (SAC) bases and leave the country unable to respond in kind. The conclusion: the United States needed to catch up to the Soviet Union.

The Air Force used the missile gap as justification for expanding its strategic arsenal; the missile manufacturers used it to bolster sales; and the Democrats seized upon it as a powerful issue for the upcoming 1960 presidential elections. In November 1958 Senator John F. Kennedy (D-Massachusetts) charged that the missile gap was caused by the Eisenhower administration placing fiscal policy ahead of national security.[19]

The U.S. Air Force was already advancing its ICBM program in the middle 1950s by developing the Atlas missile. The program's national priority is seen in the explosive growth in the number of people employed on the project. Though defense contractor Convair had only ten people working on the Atlas missile program in 1953, by 1960, the number had increased to twelve thousand.[20] The air force wanted at least 120 Atlas missiles operational by 1960. The public outcry for increased weapons production after Sputnik pushed those numbers even higher.[21]

Built for speed, distance, accuracy and destruction, the Atlas missile was an impressive weapon to behold. The Atlas was 82.5 feet long and 10 feet wide. It weighed 18,104 pounds empty and 267,136 pounds fueled. Its range was between 6,400 and 9,000 miles, it was accurate within 2 nautical miles, and its nuclear warhead delivered a 4-megaton yield. The air force built six versions of the Atlas missile—the A, B and C were test models, and the D, E and F were deployed for field operation. During flight, the missile reached a height of 763 miles and a speed of 16,000 miles per hour, and it traveled 6,788 miles in 43 minutes.[22] Though earlier versions of the Atlas were successfully launched in the late 1950s, "[t]he first successful launch of a Series F Atlas ICBM took place at Cape Canaveral, Florida," on August 8, 1961. Only the Atlas F missile was stored in and launched from "hardened underground silo-lift launchers."[23]

Missile deployment was also fast. Circumstances required a crash missile deployment program to safeguard the United States against the Soviet Union.

> *The hallmark of the Atlas deployment schedule was urgency; escalating tensions with the Soviet Union sent the Air Force scrambling to deploy the missiles as rapidly as possible....Originally the location of the launch sites was determined exclusively by the missile's range; they had to be within 5,000 miles of their targets in the Soviet Union. Later, other factors that influenced the placement of the sites was that they be inland, out of range of Soviet submarine-launched intermediate range missiles; close to support facilities; and as a cost cutting measure, be built on government property whenever possible.*[24]

The Atlas F missile, the type to be maintained near Altus Air Force Base, was the most advanced ICBM. Each was stored vertically in a "hard" underground silo 174 feet deep with a diameter of 52 feet. "The walls of the silo were built of heavily reinforced concrete. Within the silo the missile and its support system were supported by a steel framework called the crib, which

The Manitou Atlas F missile, pictured on June 30, 1962. *Courtesy of http://www.siloworld.net.*

hung from the walls of the silo on four sets of huge springs." An underground launch control center (LCC) was connected to each silo by a 50-foot tunnel. Also built with reinforced concrete, each control center was 27 feet high and had a diameter of 40 feet. Its two floors housed the launching equipment and served as the living quarters for the five-man launch crew.[25] The missile was raised by an elevator from its protective concrete cocoon through the massive concrete doors that were flush with the ground, after which it was fueled and launched. Although the Altus-area missile sites were among the most expensive to build, they were the least vulnerable to Soviet attack.[26]

Six Atlas F squadrons of twelve missile launch sites each were deployed near air force bases in Schilling, Kansas; Lincoln, Nebraska; Dyess, Texas; Walker, New Mexico; Plattsburg, New York; and Altus.[27] U.S. senators Robert Kerr and A.S. Mike Monroney and Congressman Toby Morris announced that Altus Air Force Base would be the hub of twelve Atlas F sites in January 1960. Then, in "April, the Corps of Engineers, Tulsa District awarded the basic construction contract to Morrison-Knudsen and Hardeman and Associates. The two firms had submitted a combined bid of just over $20.9 million."[28]

Altus Air Force Base was built during World War II and hosted flight training for pilots. After the war, it served as the municipal airport until the early 1950s. Strategic Air Command assumed control of the base in 1953, and the 11th Bombardment Wing, renamed the 11th Strategic Aerospace Wing, was assigned to Altus in September 1957. The Atlas missile was "added to the weapon inventory of Altus as part of the wing's global striking power. The Atlas was assigned to the 577th Strategic Missile Squadron which was activated…June 1, 1961."[29]

The air force turned to the Army Corps of Engineers to build both the Atlas missile launch sites and the necessary supporting facilities. The Corps of Engineers, in turn, assigned the building of these to several engineer districts.[30] Another change was made in August 1960, when the Corps of Engineers Ballistic Missile Construction Office (CEBMCO) was established to manage the massive undertaking and oversee building the individual missile sites scattered around the country. A CEBMCO area office was located at each missile site, including Altus Air Force Base, to directly oversee construction.[31]

Because of the underground depth of each silo and overall size of each launch facility, the Atlas F facilities were the most difficult to build; the task was monumental.

Construction began with an open cut excavation down to a depth of 60 feet, the level of the launch control center floor; from there the silo wall was mined to its final depth. During the mining operation the contractors supported the silo walls with steel beams, wire mesh lagging, and sprayed-on concrete. Within the silo workers then built a huge steel framework, equivalent in size to a 15-story building, to support the missile and all of its ancillary equipment.[32]

The Altus Area Office of the U.S. Army Corps of Engineers was born on March 14, 1960. Responsibility for building the office and the ICBM sites was transferred from the U.S. Army Engineer District in Tulsa to the Los Angeles CEBMCO headquarters. "By the end of October 1960 the number of personnel assigned to the Area office reached its zenith with 7 Corps of Engineers officers and 170 Department of the Army civilians."[33]

The influx of personnel associated with the missile sites in 1960 created a housing shortage in Altus.

To alleviate the scarcity of housing General Dynamics Astronautics (then Convair-Astronautics) entered into a lease agreement in December 1960 with a local real estate owner to rent a block of some 200 Title IX homes to GD/A, Air Force, and Army employees to include those members of the military service assigned to the missile project. Rental rates were on par with the Altus, Oklahoma area rental rates. For example, a 4-bedroom home rented for $100.00, $95.00 for a 3-bedroom and $85.00 for a 2-bedroom home. In addition if the occupant desired the use of a stove and refrigerator the cost was increased $10.00 monthly.[34]

The locations near Altus chosen for the twelve launch sites were designated by number: "#1-Lone Wolf; #2-Snyder; #3-Cache; #4-Frederick; #5-Fargo [Texas]; #6-Creta; #7-Hollis; #8-Russell; #9-Willow; #10-Hobart; #11-Manitou; #12-Granite….The prime construction contract was awarded to Morrison-Knudsen Company, Inc., and Hardeman and Associates" for the twelve sites with their combined bid of $20,926,500, which was considerably less expensive than the government's estimate of $23,686,717.[35]

The Altus Area Office oversaw construction of the twelve ICBM silos located near Altus Air Force Base. Each silo was "a highly reinforced concrete structure" with walls that varied "in thickness from 2½ feet to 9 feet." The silo was built to house an Atlas missile underground, and the top of each silo was "flush with the ground surface." The extremely heavy silo doors "operated hydraulically" and were able to "completely seal off the silo." Each silo "required over 1,800 tons of reinforcing steel and approximately 6,000 cubic yards of high strength concrete."[36]

Symbolic ground-breaking ceremony for the Atlas missile program, May 20, 1960, including the mayors of Altus and the twelve communities that hosted the sites. *Courtesy of the Old Greer County Museum, Mangum, Oklahoma.*

Needing thousands of acres for the missile sites in southwest Oklahoma and north Texas, the U.S. government exercised eminent domain and took ownership of the private land near Altus Air Force Base. "To acquire the needed 12,879 acres...the Real Estate Division of the Tulsa District filed condemnation suits against 477 landowners in the 6 counties surrounding Altus."[37] Excavation on the first Altus Air Force Base missile sites began in May 1960.[38] Amis Construction Company of Oklahoma City completed the open-cut excavation for all of the Altus-area missile sites.[39]

Constructing the missile sites was dangerous. In all, over fifty men died nationwide in site accidents, "and many more were killed in traffic accidents around the work sites."[40] Three men were killed while building the Altus Air Force Base missile sites.[41] Eight work stoppages briefly halted work at several of the Altus-area missile sites under construction. On September 8, 1960, electricians at the Lone Wolf, Snyder, Cache and Creta sites walked off the job for four days because non-electricians were used to complete some of the electrical work. Workers at the Hollis site left from October 21 until October 24, 1960, claiming that the silo ladder was unsafe to climb. Ironworkers at the Snyder site stopped work from November 4 until November 7, 1960, citing unsafe silo conditions. Unhappy with their oversight, Granite workers declined to work for one day, November 16, 1960. Alleging that ironworkers were doing plumbing work, plumbers at the Lone Wolf, Snyder, Cache, Creta, Hollis, Hobart and Manitou sites walked off the job on November 22, 1960. In a show of respect for an ironworker who was killed at the Cache site on December 28, 1960, fellow ironworkers there walked off the site that day. Because of a local dispute, several unionized laborers refused to work from April 25 through April 28,

1961. The final stoppage happened on July 5, 1961, when metalworkers at the Fargo, Texas site walked off during contract negotiations.[42]

Building the twelve Altus-area missile sites included significant labor and associated costs. "Of the prime contract, approximately $9.3 million of the cost was expended by the contractor for labor. Of this total cost, approximately $3.9 million was for overtime; $1.7 million for travel and subsistence; and $1.5 million for premium pay." Pay was awarded for 3.7 million man-hours.[43]

Jerry Brewer of Elk City was a twenty-year-old newlywed in 1961, and he needed a job. In September, he went to work at the Cache site, where he was employed by General Dynamics as a timekeeper, keeping all timesheet totals and logging them for payroll. He made $1.90 an hour. "The federal minimum wage was $1.15 then, so what I made was good pay."[44] In early 1962, Brewer transferred to the Granite site, where he worked for Fluor as an operating engineer. "General Dynamics was the contractor, and Fluor was the sub-contractor," he explained. His shift rotated weekly, and because he joined the International Union of Operating Engineers, he earned $3.00 an hour on the day shift, $3.10 an hour for the evening shift and $3.15 an hour working the night shift. His job was to maintain the equipment that ran around the clock for construction. "Fluor had inspectors, General Dynamics had inspectors, and the air force had inspectors. Work had to pass all three, with the air force having the final say." By the time his Granite missile site job ended in September 1962, he had saved enough money to pay the local hospital the $200 for the birth of his firstborn son and provide a down payment on the $7,650 Elk City house that he and his wife bought.[45]

Local media covered construction of the twelve Altus Air Force Base Atlas missile sites. According to *History of the Altus Area Office* by S.C. Wood for the U.S. Army Corps of Engineers, between the Altus Area Office's opening until late April 1962, sixty-nine stories about missile site construction appeared in local newspapers, plus "one nationwide news release was published by the *Army Times*, Washington, D.C." A Lawton television station also featured construction of the local missile sites:

> *On 2 July 1961 the Area Engineer appeared in a 45 minute panel discussion on KSWO-TV, Lawton, Oklahoma. Other members of the panel were Colonel Ernest L. Ramme, USAF, Altus SATAF Commander; Lt Col R.E. Jarrell, USAF, Deputy Commander, 577th Strategic Missile Squadron and Mr. J.N. McPheeters, Altus Manager, General Dynamics/ Astronautics. The panel discussed the construction of the Atlas F ICBM Complexes in the Altus Area.*[46]

Americans too young to remember the Cold War may not be able to understand the nationwide fear of a Soviet nuclear attack, but the fear was real. Strategic Air Command prepared for a Soviet offensive by placing one-tenth, then one-third, of its bombers on alert at all times. Additionally, SAC strategy called for twelve armed B-52s to be in the air constantly, prepared to bomb the Soviet Union should war come. Each B-52 took off in the direction of a "specified 'go or no-go' line" hundreds of miles away from the Soviet Union. "Upon reaching that imaginary line, if no authenticated order to attack was received from the American President, the bombers would turn around, refuel, and head for home….These flights typically would last about twenty-four hours," and during the return trip, "another bomber would take off to assume the alert duties of the returning craft."[47]

A national civil defense program was implemented to train Americans to prepare for a nuclear attack. Oklahoma even participated in a nationwide civil defense mock attack in May 1960. According to the results of the fictional hydrogen bomb attack, only 10 percent of Altus-area residents remained alive, and more casualties were expected among those survivors due to radiation exposure. "Civil Defense authorities said one bomb hit near Martha and another southwest of Altus near the missile site not yet built."[48]

The May 8, 1960 edition of the *Altus Times-Democrat* carried a front-page story about the downing of American pilot Francis Gary Powers while flying a U-2 spy plane on a reconnaissance mission over the Soviet Union a week earlier. The story relays that Soviet premier Nikita Khrushchev announced that Powers "was a $2,500-a-month agent of the U.S. intelligence agency and he recommended he be tried for espionage."[49]

A day after informing its readers that Francis Gary Powers was in Soviet custody, the *Altus Times-Democrat* announced that work had begun at the Lone Wolf missile site. "First earth on the No. 1 site for the $63 million Atlas ICBM project in the Altus area was moved at 10 a.m. today with several key figures assigned to the gigantic project on hand for the occasion." The newspaper described the site's location as "just east of SH 41 between Lake Altus and Lone Wolf." Work was also to begin at the Snyder and Cache sites the same day. "There were 10 construction workers at the Lone Wolf site this morning but officials said that number would be up to about 60 by the end of the week," when around-the-clock work would begin.[50]

Missile site construction brought several business offices to Altus, including Cloverland Construction Company and U.S. Engineering Company of Kansas City; Gillmore-Skouvye Company of Oakland, California; Cyclone Fencing Company of Fort Worth; and Amis Company of Oklahoma City.[51]

Left: The launch control center entrance of an Atlas F missile silo in southwest Oklahoma as it appears today. *Courtesy of the author.*

Right: This underground blast door inside a southwest Oklahoma Atlas F missile site, as it appears today, was built to withstand a nuclear blast at the surface. *Courtesy of the author.*

The July 18, 1960 *Altus Times-Democrat* announced the arrival of the Convair office in conjunction with the project. "Convair Astronautics prepared to open its Altus office today with the arrival of key officials to pave the way for a gradual buildup of a peak force of almost 1,400 company personnel whose job will be to serve as surviellance [*sic*] teams for the $63 million Altus Air Force Base ICBM project."[52]

The Altus area missile sites were built as President Eisenhower's tenure was ending and the two men vying to be his successor in the White House were battling each other on the campaign trail. The September 26, 1960 edition of the *Altus Times-Democrat* carried a front-page story about the first ever televised presidential debate, between John Kennedy and Richard Nixon, to be held that night. The same edition carried several pictures of the Snyder Atlas silo under construction, illustrating the immensity of the massive undertaking.[53]

Democratic presidential candidate John Kennedy visited Oklahoma just days before the 1960 election. Met by a raucous crowd of supporters who

The tunnel connecting the launch control center to the silo at a southwest Oklahoma Atlas missile site as it appears today. *Courtesy of the author.*

listened to him discuss "the religious issue," Kennedy was introduced by a fellow U.S. senator, Oklahoma's Robert S. Kerr. "Kerr, a millionaire Baptist layman, said he had been raised to 'love my church and believe in its doctrine' and then shouted: 'I support a patriotic Catholic Democrat for president of the United States.' " Kerr predicted that Kennedy would win the Sooner State. Republican state chairman Henry Bellmon forecast a Nixon victory in Oklahoma and criticized the Kennedy rally. "They are putting on something like they were pushing a new brand fo [*sic*] soap." Bellmon also charged that the Kennedy team "had to make telephone calls and run advertisements for days to get out a crowd. Electing a president is far more serious business than selling soap."[54]

The same day that Kennedy's Oklahoma visit was front-page news, the *Altus Times-Democrat* reported that the first missile site construction fatality had occurred at the Hobart site. Construction worker Otis S. Hopson, age thirty-one, of Lampasas, Texas, was electrocuted when a cable at the end of the crane that he was operating touched a high-voltage power line. J.D. Wright, who was standing near Hopson when he was electrocuted, was taken to the Hobart hospital, where he recovered from burns. Hobart doctors tried unsuccessfully to save Hopson on the scene. Hopson and Wright had recently finished work at the Willow site and were preparing to start work at Hobart. The day Hopson died was both men's first day there; each had been at the site less than thirty minutes when tragedy struck.[55]

The *Altus Times-Democrat* reported the December 28, 1960 death of Warren Neal Willis of DeQueen, Arkansas, while working at the Cache missile site. Willis was working in the silo and fell about one hundred feet. An ambulance took Willis to a Lawton hospital, where he was pronounced dead. Two of Willis's brothers also worked at the site. Willis, age twenty-nine, had worked at the Cache site for about three months.[56]

The *Altus Times-Democrat* carried several stories about the April 1961 Bay of Pigs Invasion, which occurred within President Kennedy's first hundred days in office. "Rebels Swarming Ashore 90 Miles outside Havana," "Rusk Declares Invaders not from U.S. Soil," "Castro Declares Emergency State as Invaders Hit" and "Cuba Charges U.S.-Financed" were some of the headlines in the April 17 edition. April 18 headlines included "Nikita Calls on Kennedy to 'Halt' Rebels in Cuba" and "Navy Clamps Security on Guantanamo."[57] This international embarrassment for President Kennedy was a prelude to a nuclear showdown with the Soviet Union over Cuba eighteen months later in which Oklahoma's missile sites would be prominently featured.

About six weeks after the Bay of Pigs, the Army Corps of Engineers transferred control of the first completed missile site launch control center at the Snyder site to the air force during a ceremony marking the transfer. The *Altus-Times Democrat* described the LCC as "a circular, two-level concrete structure about 30 feet high and buried under nine feet of earth." Similar to the silo, the LCC's floors "are suspended within their two-foot thick concrete walls" that could "absorb shock in case of a blast above the surface." The first floor of the launch control center included "living quarters for the crews which will man the Atlas around the clock," which even included a kitchen and shower. The LCC's second floor contained "the intricate consoles which ready the missile for firing and send it on its way should the need ever arise."[58]

By June 1, 1961, an extensive network of cables stretching more than two hundred miles had been established, allowing communication between Altus Air Force Base and the LCCs at the missile sites. Silo doors were added to the twelve Altus Air Force Base missile sites toward the end of construction. Though extremely heavy, the concrete-and-steel doors through which the Atlas was raised from beneath by an elevator could open quickly. LCCs at the remaining sites also were being prepared for transfer to the air force that summer.[59]

The Atlas missile program was launched to deter a Soviet nuclear attack and, if necessary, retaliate against that nation. The U.S. government took steps to save American lives in the event that deterrence failed. The August 1, 1961 *Altus Times-Democrat* carried a front-page story about Secretary of Defense Robert McNamara's appearance before Congress to pitch President Kennedy's civil defense plan for creating shelters to protect Americans from a nuclear attack. McNamara told Congress that President Kennedy's plan to create shelters from radioactive fallout could save up to fifteen million lives. The goal was to provide enough shelter for fifty million people, which was about 25 percent of the country's population.[60]

The same edition of the Altus newspaper also reported that the Snyder missile silo had been transferred to the air force. "In a ceremony somewhat longer than it takes an ICBM to zoom out of sight, the construction phase of the Atlas launching complex at Snyder was declared officially over today." The remaining sites would follow suit and "be ready for signing over to the Air Force and become available for General Dynamics–Astronautics to start installation and check-out work at each site." The story forecast that 2,500 workers would be needed, and their work would continue through the following year.[61] The Snyder ceremony was attended by civic leaders including state senator Ryan Kerr and state house member Maurice Willis, both of Altus; Altus mayor Hoyt Shadid; and Snyder mayor William Fulps. Snyder Chamber of Commerce president Dr. E.A. Allgood and Altus Chamber of Commerce president Coy Shadid were among the business leaders present.[62]

The Snyder launching complex alone "required the removal of 60,000 yards of earth, pouring of 6,900 yards of concrete and the use of over 537 tons of steel" by crews who worked twenty-four hours a day. "When operational, the launching complex is an underground city within itself, capable of producing its own electrical current, water and sewage disposal." The silo could have held "over 2½ million gallons of water, and enough concrete was used in each of the complexes to pave 30 city blocks with a six inch layer."[63]

America's greatest fears were nearly realized as the Cold War entered its most dangerous two-week span in October 1962 when the United States discovered that the Soviet Union was placing nuclear missiles ninety miles from Florida, triggering the Cuban missile crisis. "Potentially Hot Showdown

An Atlas missile being delivered to an Altus-area missile silo. *Courtesy of the Old Greer County Museum, Mangum, Oklahoma.*

Nearing; Russia Claims U.S. Sets Stage for War" was the front page headline of the October 23, 1962 *Altus Times-Democrat.*[64]

The first Atlas F ICBM in the Altus Air Force Base arsenal was put on alert status two months before the Cuban crisis. The remaining eleven missiles followed suit in October. "As a result of the Cuban missile crisis during the latter part of the month, the Series F Atlas squadrons at...Altus (577th)... were for the first time required to place all 12 missiles on alert."[65]

The day after President Kennedy addressed the nation about the Cuban crisis, the *Altus Times-Democrat* reported that Altus Air Force Base had no comment when asked if the base had been placed on heightened alert. The newspaper also reported that Altus Air Force Base had, the previous week, "become one of three Atlas 'F' missile launching points now operational in the nation," at which time the 577th Strategic Missile Squadron at Altus Air Force Base had assumed control of all twelve missile sites.[66]

In response to the Cuban crisis, Jackson County Civil Defense officials met with city and county leaders as well as Altus Air Force Base personnel to

Front page of the October 23, 1962 edition of the *Daily Oklahoman. Courtesy of the author.*

plan for a possible attack. Jackson County Civil Defense director Tal Oden said that a pair of siren blasts, each lasting three minutes, would warn locals to monitor television or radio. A continual siren blast meant that an attack was imminent, and residents should seek immediate shelter. Oden stressed the planning necessary for families to survive a nuclear attack by choosing a safe place to take refuge and by gathering provisions and medical products.[67]

Fortunately, disaster was averted, and the crisis was resolved peacefully in late October. However, as international tensions relaxed, local tensions heightened as Oklahomans near Cache received a scare when a liquid oxygen tank at the missile site there began leaking. The tank was drained by the base disaster team, and any threat was eliminated, but the sight of mist that appeared to be smoke, along with the appearance of the base team working with firefighting equipment, fueled a rumor in the area that the Atlas missile complex was on fire.[68] Another dangerous incident occurred when the Atlas missile stored at the Frederick site exploded shortly before noon on May 14, 1964. No injuries resulted, and fortunately, the nuclear warhead was unaffected. State and local law enforcement evacuated and secured the area, and locals were instructed to avoid the scene as investigators worked to determine the explosion's cause and to assess the damage.[69]

On November 19, 1964, Secretary of Defense McNamara, who since the November 1963 assassination of President Kennedy answered to President Lyndon Johnson, announced that the Atlas F missiles would be "phased out…by the end of June 1965." And on March 25, 1965, the 577th Strategic Missile Squadron was deactivated. Southwest Oklahoma's part in the nation's missile program ended.[70]

Most of the launch facilities, built at breakneck speed around the country during the most intense and dangerous period of the Cold War, sit empty and unused. After the Atlas missiles were decommissioned and phased out, the military declared that the missile sites were surplus and subject to sale through the General Services Administration.[71] All twelve of the Altus-area missile sites were sold to private owners.[72]

In 1999, David Johnson bought the abandoned Atlas F missile site west of Hobart from its owner on the Internet, intending to turn the Cold War–era Kiowa County LCC into a home. In a 2009 story, the *Oklahoman* reported that "the government has helped seal off a couple of the old silos, filling them with concrete and welding the doors shut." Richard Guinan, historian for the Ninety-Seventh Air Mobility Wing, attributed the Atlas missile program's termination to the May 1964 explosion at the Frederick missile site. "That was one of several incidents in the Air Force, but that was the last straw. After the Frederick missile silo site exploded, they started shutting the program down." Some of the silos were donated to area schools, "and many area school districts—Snyder, Hollis, Granite, and Northside High School near Fargo, Texas—still use the land, having placed FFA barns or other such ag-ed facilities and equipment at the sites."[73] Guinan had the opportunity to visit the Hobart silo, and he was taken aback. "You see things you don't read about, about how there's so many turns from the top door….The size and the quality of the work, the concrete walls, everything still looks new." He reflected on the bygone era that the silo represented. "When you walk into his complex and just look around, it takes you back to a time when the nation had a different threat…the end-of-the-world threat, nuclear attack."[74]

Because of missile technology advances, the Atlas was soon considered obsolete. Ironically, the danger posed by the Cold War made building the Atlas missile sites as quickly as possible imperative, yet the same danger caused the United States to abandon them for a more advanced missile just as quickly.[75]

Historians generally agree that the Cuban missile crisis was the closest that the world has come to nuclear war. On the evening of October 22, 1962, in the middle of the crisis, President Kennedy spoke to the nation in a televised Oval Office address explaining the situation in Cuba. He told the American public that the United States would "regard any nuclear missile launched from Cuba against any nation in the Western Hemisphere as an attack by the Soviet Union on the United States, requiring a full retaliatory response against the Soviet Union." That "full retaliatory response" would have included firing the Atlas F missiles surrounding Altus Air Force Base.[76]

The Atlas missile program was needed to deter a Soviet nuclear attack and to defend the United States if deterrence failed. The program was a national security priority spanning the presidencies of Eisenhower, Kennedy and Johnson from the late 1950s through 1965. Southwest Oklahoma played a crucial role in the nation's Cold War nuclear arsenal by building the Atlas F missile sites and housing those missiles during the most dangerous years of the decades-long conflict between the United States and the Soviet Union. The missiles of Oklahoma near Altus Air Force Base provided jobs, created an economic boon for southwest Oklahoma and, most importantly, kept all Americans safe during the most dangerous period in the history of this nation—and the world.

A MISSILE TECHNICIAN'S EXPERIENCE

The best decision that Jerry Burns ever made was joining the U.S. Air Force. Following a colorful elementary and high school career admittedly short on academic achievement, life got sweeter for the twenty-year-old Covington, Kentucky, native when he took the plunge on February 14, 1961, and formally joined. After completing six weeks of basic training at Lackland Air Force Base in Texas, Burns transferred to Sheppard Air Force Base, where he completed a nearly year-long technical school ending in early 1962. "The USAF had selected me to be a BMAT (Ballistic Missile Analyst Technician) on an Atlas-F ICBM launch crew," Burns said. This assignment would bring him to southwest Oklahoma.[77] Burns spent almost a year at Sheppard Air Force Base learning to be a ballistic missile analyst technician. According to Burns, the school was the U.S. Air Force's most thorough and extensive technician program then. He said that it was tough, but it was also worth enduring. "I knew that missile and the silo from top to bottom when I graduated," Burns said, "and I was always comfortable in my job." He left the school as an airman second class (E-3) and went to Altus, Oklahoma, for his first posting after technician school. He would spend the rest of 1962 through 1965 at Altus Air Force Base with the 577th Strategic Missile Squadron.[78]

"I was the…BMAT on Atlas-F ICBM Launch Crew R-43, from the time that the squadron went operational until it was deactivated," Burns said. Burns and his crew would work twenty-four hours inside the missile silo, then be off two days. "Of course, those 'off' days were usually filled with training, but I was smart in those days, so I ate it up." He enjoyed the type of duty and schedule so much that he reenlisted after four years.[79]

At twenty-one, Burns was an integral part of an Altus-area ICBM launch crew for the U.S. Air Force. Because of technology and training, he and his crew could ready an Atlas F for launch in ten minutes. Though slow by today's standards, ten minutes to fire a missile was considered rapid in the early 1960s. "Thankfully, that never happened," Burns said. But he and his crew came awfully close to firing one.[80]

Each crew that operated an Atlas F missile was made up of two officers and three enlistees. "Our 24 hr tours on alert were pressure-packed," Burns said. After being delivered to the site by helicopter and going through a change-over briefing, the crew would continually inspect both the launch control center and the eight-level silo that housed the missile. Burns loved this. "Maybe it was because I knew my job forward and backward, and it felt good to be so confident," he said. Burns and his crew slept and ate inside the underground launch control center. "There were bunks, kitchen facilities, showers," he said. "All of the comforts of home."[81]

Part of operating the missile was conducting launch simulations to be prepared to fire it. A launch sequence included testing the electronics, placing twenty-five thousand gallons of liquid oxygen (LOX) in the missile and raising it through the silo doors into launch position using an elevator. Large diesel generators located on levels five and six of the silo provided the power for the elevator. Though kerosene was stored inside the missile, the liquid oxygen, which was stored at the bottom of the silo on level eight, had to be transferred, which could be dangerous. "If the LOX mixed with any hydrocarbon, you had a 'bomb.'" Pictures of the Atlas raised usually show steam or smoke coming from the top of the missile, caused by liquid oxygen boiling off, which it did "continuously at ambient temperatures."[82]

The U.S. military has established five defense conditions, with DEFCON 5 being the state of readiness during peacetime. Each successive state means that the United States is closer to war until reaching DEFCON 1, "Maximum force readiness," meaning the country is at war. For the first time in its existence, Strategic Air Command's bases were placed on DEFCON 2—one step short of nuclear war—during the Cuban missile crisis in October 1962.[83]

Burns's crew was on duty during the crisis when SAC was placed on DEFCON 2. "In fact, the Missile Combat Crew Commander (MCCC) and I were on the console and decoded that Alert message from SAC Headquarters," Burns said. "It went something like: 'Skybird, Skybird, this is Looking Glass with a Red Dot Two message.' " Burns said that he realized that this was an authentic order, not a drill. He readied his Atlas missile to fire, which included a countdown, "up to 'Commit,' " which, in his words, meant "that we were just one more button, and two minutes away from WWIII….I guess the world will never really understand how close we came that night." Burns and his crew even considered bringing their families to the underground silo for their protection if nuclear war started.[84]

In 1964, while Burns was at Altus Air Force Base, the air force solicited volunteers for helicopter flight training. Burns volunteered, but because of poor vision, he was denied admission to the program. According to Burns, five others from Altus Air Force Base were accepted and shipped to Vietnam after their training. All five of them died there.[85]

4

ATLAS SHRIEKED

THE FREDERICK SITE EXPLOSION

Chapter 2 mentions the May 14, 1964, explosion at the Frederick, Oklahoma, Atlas missile site, which motivated the Department of Defense to rapidly phase out the Atlas program. This chapter gives details surrounding the explosion.

Major Casimir Harazda was the missile combat crew commander on duty when the explosion happened. As MCCC, Harazda commanded the five-man air force crew at Frederick that day and held one of the two keys required for missile launch. The deputy missile combat crew commander (DMCCC) held the other. One day several years after the accident, Harazda found a recording of the explosion that someone had mysteriously left for him in audio tape format in a foot locker. He does not know the source of the audio tape. He transferred the audio to compact disc, and that audio is available at the *Atlas Missile Silo* website.[86]

The audio includes a narration of events leading up to and including the explosion, mostly by Major Ray McAllister. McAllister was responsible for overseeing that day's propellant load exercise (PLX), a test of the missile that included loading fuel onto the missile and raising it in preparation for launch. The test was performed without a warhead in the missile. The routine test went awry, and the missile exploded, destroying the site. The force of the explosion threw the sixty-five-ton concrete silo doors off their hinges. The Atlas missile site at Frederick was closed because of this explosion and remained closed until the Atlas program was phased out nearly a year later.[87]

Major Harazda provided the audio of that day's events and the following letter to the website administrator:

TO WHOM IT MAY CONCERN

This reel to reel tape was made at the 577th standboard room at Altus AFB. I suppose that this was standard procedure during a wet countdown. The person who is narrating the countdown is Maj. Ray A McAllister, the sector commander. The wet countdown was to serve as an acceptance of the silo from the General Dynamics company who were upgrading the missile system under operation Red Heat. Our crew was scheduled for duty that day, May 14, 1964.

The crew was:

MCCC   Maj. Casimir J. Harazda, AO2084560
DMCC   1Lt. Keith N. Kuhlenschmidt, AO3107988
BMT   MSgt. P-2 William C. Smith, AF14299145
MFT   SSgt. Donald P. Huelle, AF19523242
EPPT   A1C George E. Ellis, AF37636589

As I remember there were two minor corrections I would like to make to the tape. When it appeared to me that the fire indication on the Missile Facilities Panel was not a false one I instructed the DMCC to initiate the fire fog system, but the green light did not come on. Also later on I suggested that the missile silo doors should be opened. A GD engineer negated the idea. Later on the tape, someone on the conference net suggests that the fog system be initiated, where we informed Maj. McAllister that an attempt was made earlier and it did not activate. Later someone else on the net suggested that we open the missile silo doors to relieve the blast force. It was almost too late. After I activated the open door sequence and when both doors were just partially extended we lost both diesels and all power to the silo. Several minutes later the missile exploded and the resulting blast blew each door several feet away from their hinges.

The sudden silence at the end of the tape was because I ordered every one to the first level of the LCC where the escape hatch was. Fortunately, we did not have to use it and we all exited from the normal entry and exit way. I was the last one to leave the silo.

As a final remark I would like to add that during the LOX loading I never saw the frost line come up towards the top of the missile through observation of the remote camera in the MEA. I believe this was significant since a leak of some kind was suspected at the missile lox connection. I'm not sure that this was proven.

[Signed]
Casimir J. Harazda[88]

5

BEARING WITNESS

earning about the missiles of Oklahoma was both professionally satisfying and a lot of fun. I grew up in western Oklahoma, yet I knew almost nothing about the Atlas missile sites until I was forty. I decided that this history needed to be preserved and the public needed to know about it. I did this by writing, speaking and placing a historic marker. My speaking about these missile sites included presentations to several civic organizations and on college campuses in Oklahoma and Texas.

I spoke to the Kiwanis Club and Rotary Club in Elk City; the Kiwanis Club and Rotary Club in Sayre; the Rotary Club in Shamrock, Texas; the Rotary Club in Weatherford; and at the Elk City Carnegie Library. Additionally, I spoke at the annual banquet of the Kiowa County Historical Society in Hobart, and I was the featured speaker for the Stafford Air & Space Museum series Stories at the Stafford in Weatherford.

In October 2017, Southwestern Oklahoma State University sponsored a two-night Missiles of Oklahoma seminar in conjunction with the fifty-fifth anniversary of the Cuban missile crisis, in which Oklahoma's missiles played a prominent role. To say that this was a thrill is an understatement.

I spoke first on the evening of October 16 at the Sayre campus, where I teach. The second night of the seminar was held on October 26 at the Weatherford campus, where I was joined by Michael Dobbs, author of *One Minute to Midnight: Kennedy, Khrushchev, and Castro on the Brink of Nuclear War*.[89]

Dobbs, SWOSU president Randy Beutler and I had spent most of that day together. Our itinerary included a guided tour of one of Southwest

Oklahoma's Atlas missile sites, which its owner—and our tour guide—has renovated and lives in. It was the second time I had viewed this site, and it was as fascinating as the first visit had been the previous June, when I was accompanied by my father. Dad was keenly interested in my research, because he'd worked at the Cache and Granite missile sites while they were under construction in the early 1960s.

Placing a historic marker at one of the Oklahoma missile sites was personally gratifying. During the process of researching and writing about the Atlas missile sites near Altus Air Force Base, I decided that at least one of the sites deserved public recognition. The Oklahoma Historical Society provided me the application for a historic marker. I secured permission from the property owner, submitted all of the required paperwork and was approved to place a state-sponsored historic marker at the Atlas missile site near Willow in Greer County.

Because of budgetary constraints, I was responsible for raising the funds necessary to purchase and place the marker, so I partnered with the Old Greer County Museum and Hall of Fame in Mangum. I'm glad I did. Museum director Stephen Dock enthusiastically supported the project, and he was instrumental in raising the necessary funds. Stephen distributes a museum newsletter, and he mentioned the missile site historic marker fundraising project in one edition after we'd begun receiving a few donations from interested entities in western Oklahoma. Readers Charles and Mary Ellen Doyle generously offered to pay for the entire marker. The marker arrived from Ohio, where it was created, and I oversaw its installation on October 25, 2017. Below is the text that I provided for the historic marker, which sits about one hundred yards west of the Willow Atlas missile site beside Oklahoma Highway 34/U.S. Highway 283 in Greer County:

To counter the Soviet Union's Cold War nuclear threat in the 1950s, the United States government created the Atlas Intercontinental Ballistic Missile. Twelve Atlas F Missile sites were built near Altus Air Force Base between 1960 and 1962. One of these sites sat immediately east of this marker.

The underground silo that housed the 82-foot-long missile here was 174 feet deep with a diameter of 52 feet. Connected to the missile silo by a tunnel was the underground Launch Control Center. A five-person crew lived there around the clock, ready to fire the missile. Once fired, the Atlas stored here was capable of reaching the Soviet Union in 43 minutes.

This missile site was attached to the 577th Strategic Missile Squadron at Altus Air Force Base. All 12 Altus-area missiles were put on alert during

The historic marker placed by the author near the Willow Atlas missile site in 2017. *Courtesy of the author.*

the October 1962 Cuban Missile Crisis. On March 25, 1965, the 577th SMS was inactivated.

The Atlas Missile program was a national security priority under Presidents Eisenhower, Kennedy and Johnson. The Willow Atlas Missile site played a crucial role in the nation's Cold War nuclear arsenal from 1962 to 1965. This marker provided by the CHARLES T. and MARY ELLEN DOYLE FAMILY.

Before all of the funds were raised for the marker, I had the opportunity to appear on a segment of "Is This a Great State or What?" on KFOR NewsChannel 4 in Oklahoma City. Photojournalist Galen Culver and I visited the Granite and Willow missile sites in June 2017—after I spoke that day at the Elk City Rotary Club about the missiles of Oklahoma—and he shot footage of me as I discussed those sites.[90] My missile site travels included a trip to the University of Texas in Austin. I presented the poster "Oklahoma Missile Site: Aiming for the Historic Marker" about the Willow historic marker project at the annual meeting of the American Association for State and Local History on September 8, 2017.

I interviewed my father for this book, and I asked him to give me details about his memories of working at the Cache and Granite missile sites while they were under construction. The day after Christmas, 2016, my two youngest children, Dad and I drove from Elk City to Willow and walked the grounds of the missile site there. This was my first time visiting any of

Above: The silo pad and silo doors at the Granite missile site. *Courtesy of the author.*

Right: U.S. Army Corps of Engineers survey mark in the concrete pad at the Granite missile site. *Courtesy of the author.*

the Atlas missile sites. My excitement was childlike. Dad, my sons and I walked the grounds, spotted the silo pad and doors, the above-ground LCC entrance and the remaining Quonset hut. And I took lots of pictures. Then we drove to the Granite site, walked those grounds and took lots of pictures. This was the first time that Dad had been to the Granite site since his last day on the job fifty-three years earlier, just before the site was turned over to the air force. I asked Dad to describe his memories that were stirred by driving the same road south one hundred yards or so from Highway 9 to the silo and being there that day. This is what he said:

> *Just driving onto the Granite site, up the same road I took on each shift. I thought of the men I worked with, the smell and sound of diesel engines turning the huge generators, the vapor rising from liquid oxygen pipes, driving the seventy miles round trip from Elk City to Granite to work each of my shifts, the "clangs" of ironworkers constructing the site, and the danger that was always present when we descended into the silo.*

It's interesting that Dad mentioned the danger. After all, three men died while building the Altus-area missile sites—one was electrocuted at the Hobart site; one fell to his death at the Cache site, where Dad had worked; and another fell to his death at the Fargo, Texas site on March 24, 1961. The Altus newspaper reported that construction worker Keith Arnold was preparing for concrete to be poured on the launch control center at the

Fargo site when he fell approximately thirty feet to his death. According to the newspaper, Arnold's pregnant wife, unaware of her husband's death, was admitted about an hour after the accident to the hospital in Vernon to give birth.

I understand why danger was always present.

Dad also said that all of his work was done from inside the silo at each site. "They [the silos] were massive—especially when at the lower levels looking up. I never felt claustrophobic, but there was always a sense of awe and a tinge of danger," Dad said.

Dad said that he worked with a sense that he and his coworkers were doing something important during their eight-hour shifts. Dad's job consisted of making sure all operating equipment (generator engines, pumps, etc.) was running smoothly and logging all of the information on their gauges. Lunch breaks meant eating in the silo. Shifts were eight hours—7:00 a.m. to 3:00 p.m., 3:00 p.m. to 11:00 p.m., and 11 p.m. to 7:00 a.m. He also worked monthly double shifts from 7:00 a.m. to 11:00 p.m.

Dad's dad, Clyde Brewer—my Papaw Clyde—worked at the Manitou missile site while it was under construction. Dad said that Papaw did the same job at Manitou that he did at Granite. Papaw worked at the Manitou site less than a year. Papaw died when I was three, so my memories of him are few and foggy. I'd heard that he and my grandmother had lived at Manitou, but I didn't know why. Now I do. Connecting these dots in family history is nice.

Among the most personally satisfying aspects of this entire missile sites venture was the historic marker dedication ceremony at the Willow site on November 10, 2017. The public was invited, and I spoke to the folks who braved the cold temperatures that were enhanced by the brisk western Oklahoma wind. Among the attendees were my parents.

Dad, my two youngest children and I had first walked the Willow site grounds nearly a year earlier, and this day, I was getting to dedicate a historic marker to educate the public and preserve this history for generations to come. And I was getting to share it with my family where it all began eleven months earlier.

Below are the remarks that I made that cold November Friday:

> *My name is Landry Brewer. I teach history for Southwestern Oklahoma State University in Sayre. October last year I began researching the twelve Cold War nuclear missile sites near Altus Air Force Base, including the one here at Willow….*

Grain storage sitting on the concrete pad atop the Willow site silo, which housed an Atlas F intercontinental ballistic missile from 1962 to 1965. *Courtesy of the author.*

Quonset hut *(left)* and above-ground launch control center entrance at the Willow Atlas missile site. *Courtesy of the author.*

Launch control center entrance *(foreground)* and grain storage sitting atop the silo that housed an Atlas F intercontinental ballistic missile at the Willow site from 1962 to 1965. *Courtesy of the author.*

During this process, I decided that at least one of the Altus-area missile sites deserved public recognition, so I petitioned the state historical society to place a historic marker here.

The Oklahoma Historical Society granted my request, and I partnered with the Old Greer County Museum in Mangum to raise the money to pay for the marker.

Like so many people in western Oklahoma, I have a personal connection to these missile sites. My dad, Jerry Brewer, worked at the Cache and Granite missile sites when they were being built in 1961 and '62. His dad, Clyde Brewer—my Papaw Clyde—worked at the Manitou missile site when it was being built. Though I'd occasionally heard Dad mention missile sites, I had no idea what he was talking about.

Then, thirteen months ago, Dad showed me a website with army documents and air force documents explaining what these missile sites were and how important they were to Southwest Oklahoma, the nation and the world.

From shortly after World War II until the early 1990s, the threat of war existed between the U.S. and the Soviet Union. It was called the Cold

Historic marker placed by the author at the Willow Atlas missile site in 2017. *Left to right, background:* the Quonset hut, launch control center entrance and grain storage sitting atop the silo that housed an Atlas F intercontinental ballistic missile from 1962 to 1965. *Courtesy of the author.*

War. Because both countries developed nuclear weapons, the Cold War was extremely dangerous. The Atlas F intercontinental ballistic missiles at Willow and eleven other locations near Altus Air Force Base were part of the American offensive nuclear arsenal during the most dangerous part of this dangerous time.

All twelve Altus-area missiles, including the one that was stored here, were on alert during the October 1962 Cuban missile crisis. Those thirteen days were the most dangerous period in the history of the world.

President Kennedy went on national television in the middle of the crisis the evening of October 22nd to explain to the nation that the Soviet Union was installing nuclear missiles in Cuba, just ninety miles south of Florida. If launched, the Soviet nuclear missiles there could have destroyed much of the United States in a matter of minutes.

If that crisis had escalated to nuclear war, the Willow missile and the other eleven missiles surrounding Altus Air Force Base would have been fired at the Soviet Union. And if the missile here had been fired, it would have reached the Soviet Union in less than forty-five minutes.

The United States dropped two atomic bombs on the Japanese cities Hiroshima and Nagasaki at the end of World War II. Those two bombs destroyed two cities and killed more than 200,000 people. The nuclear warhead inside the Atlas missile stored here at Willow was more than 200 times more powerful than those atomic bombs.

Fortunately, the missiles here and at the eleven other sites nearby were never fired. The Cold War ended in the early 1990s, and memory of those missile sites faded. But this historic marker will help all of us remember this important part of our past.

When asked in a 1992 interview why he wrote his biography of President Truman, author David McCullough said that writing about President Truman meant writing about America then. And he said that this was important because "we must be reminded who we are."

As Americans, and as Oklahomans, we must be reminded of who we are. And in the 1960s, Oklahomans built these missile sites. Oklahoma housed these missile sites. Air Force personnel in Oklahoma operated these missile sites. Oklahomans lived with these missile sites.

As Americans, and as Oklahomans, this is part of who we are. And this historic marker reminds us.

Three men died while building the Altus-area missile sites—including Otis Hopson, a thirty-one-year-old construction worker from Lampasas, Texas. He had just finished work here at the Willow site. And on his first day of work at the Hobart site, he was electrocuted.

I would like to dedicate this marker to those men. But not just to those men. I would like to dedicate this marker to all *of those who built all twelve of the Altus-area missiles sites….*

Our gathering here the day before Veterans' Day is fitting, because I would also like to dedicate this marker to the Air Force personnel who stood guard and manned these missiles. Because they kept my parents…and my grandparents…safe. Because they kept all *Oklahomans safe. Because they kept all* Americans *safe.*

And I would like to dedicate this marker to the people of Willow and Greer County and all of the other Southwest Oklahoma counties who lived with these missile sites and missiles as part of their daily lives during a scary time.

I owe a special thank-you to all of the people and organizations that made this marker possible. Thank you to the Oklahoma Historical Society for granting permission to place the marker; the Mike Clark family for allowing me to place the marker here; Stephen Dock and the Old Greer

County Museum and Hall of Fame in Mangum for partnering with me to raise the money to pay for the marker; thank you to the generous donors, including the Charles T. and Mary Ellen Doyle family; Max Post; First National Bank & Trust of Elk City; Legacy Bank of Elk City; and James and Nancy Greer; thank you to Will Snipes, Doug Kyle and William Cornell with the Oklahoma Department of Transportation; to Culver Fence Company of Elk City for installing the marker; to Southwestern Oklahoma State University president Randy Beutler, dean of the College of Arts & Sciences Peter Grant, and Sayre campus dean Sherron Manning for your support throughout this endeavor; and thank you, Dad, for passing along your love of history, and for passing along the missile site information that started me down this path of discovery thirteen months ago.

To all those I just mentioned, thank you for helping me inform the public about Southwest Oklahoma's role in keeping the world safe during the most dangerous time the world has ever known.

Thank you for helping remind us who we are.

Each Altus-area missile site cost $21 million to build. Of course, that was in 1960 dollars. Today, the price tag to build would be approximately $176 million each.

The money spent was staggering. The pace was frantic. The need was urgent.

Critics may say that spending such large sums of money for missile sites that were operational for only three years was a waste. But that's from a twenty-first-century perspective, and hindsight is always 20/20. In the context of 1960s Cold War America, the missiles of Oklahoma were a necessity to keep Americans safe by discouraging a Soviet nuclear attack. Remember, we came to the brink of nuclear war in October 1962 when the missiles were part of the nation's arsenal. Nikita Khrushchev knew our offensive capability, which discouraged a Soviet attack.

Additionally, that the missiles were never fired is the ultimate success of the weapon. It was better to have them and not need them than to need them and not have them. Nuclear war was averted, and our parents, grandparents and great-grandparents lived to tell us about it.

Sure, my family benefitted financially by the sites being built. They provided my father and grandfather jobs when jobs weren't easy to come by. But my gratitude is primarily because the sites kept my parents and grandparents and everybody else safe. And learning about them has been pretty cool. Especially the stories.

A former SWOSU colleague told me that she grew up in Southwest Oklahoma, and she was a small child when the missile sites were being built. She said that as a little girl, she was very scared of them.

The Willow site property owner told me that the silo was filled in about fifteen years ago with a sand and concrete mixture, and the silo doors were closed and sealed. Before then, the doors were open, and the silo was accessible. One of my nontraditional college students told of visiting the Willow site when she was a child. She said that she peered over the edge of the silo, which frightened her. She said that her brother climbed inside and played in it.

A friend told me that when he was a western Oklahoma high school student in the 1980s, he and a classmate went to the Willow silo, climbed in and explored. The Willow site property owner told me in 2016 that teenagers used to do that, which was motivation to fill in the silo and seal the doors.

The stories, the people, the importance—the missiles of Oklahoma represent world, national, state and local history all rolled into one. For me, they're also part of my family history, and they provided an opportunity for an intergenerational experience that connected my grandfather and my youngest children that I wouldn't trade.

6
SOONER STATE CIVIL DEFENSE

As the Cold War moved into the nuclear age and tensions with the Soviet Union heightened, all Americans, including Oklahomans, learned to live with the threat of nuclear war. To increase the likelihood of survival if nuclear war came, national, state and local civil defense organizations took steps to protect the public. As "preparedness" became the nation's watchword, the state's communities and college campuses prepared for the worst during the Cold War's hottest years.

In light of the Soviet Union's breaking the American atomic monopoly and acquiring an atomic bomb in 1949, Congress passed, and President Truman signed into law, the Federal Civil Defense Act of 1950, creating the Federal Civil Defense Administration (FCDA). To protect Americans against a Soviet attack, the FCDA envisioned "a three-stage shelter program which would (1) locate existing shelter, (2) upgrade potential shelter, and (3) construct new shelter in deficit areas in the Nation's 'critical target cities' as designated by the FCDA and the Department of Defense."[91]

President Eisenhower believed that while the federal government could provide guidance for civil defense, the bulk of those responsibilities lay with state and local governments. However, according to *Civil Defense and Homeland Security: A Short History of National Preparedness Efforts*, after learning of the extremely dangerous "blast and thermal effects" of the American hydrogen bomb detonation in 1952, the Soviet Union's hydrogen bomb detonation in 1953 and "the March 1954 BRAVO hydrogen bomb explosion," American policymakers became concerned about "the lethal hazard of long-range radioactive fallout." Many in the American government recognized the danger posed by fallout's spread over thousands of miles after a nuclear explosion, which moved Chet Holified, chair of the House Military Operations Subcommittee, to scrutinize the Eisenhower administration's civil defense policy. Representative Holified sponsored H.R. 2125, a bill to elevate civil defense to the cabinet level, emphasizing the primacy of the federal government's civil defense role and establishing a nationwide shelter system. The FCDA followed suit and proposed a $32-billion national shelter program.[92]

President Eisenhower assigned a committee to study the FCDA shelter plan in April 1957. The Security Resources Panel of the Science Advisory Committee was chaired by H. Rowan Gaither and was known popularly as the Gaither Committee. The committee made several recommendations to President Eisenhower and the National Security Council, including improving the Strategic Air Command forces, hastening development of intercontinental and intermediate-range ballistic missiles, fortifying ICBM locations, enlarging American forces and diminishing the vulnerability of American cities. The committee suggested a "passive defense" strategy featuring a $25-billion national program for nuclear fallout shelters to save lives in the event of a nuclear war. Pressure on Eisenhower mounted, caused by two momentous events that year. In August, the Soviet Union launched the first ICBM. Then, in October, the Soviets launched the first artificial satellite, Sputnik, into orbit. Eisenhower responded by merging the FCDA and the Office of Defense Mobilization to create the Office of Civil Defense Mobilization. The administration called on state and local governments to coordinate in creating a national shelter system while merely receiving "advice and guidance" from the federal government.[93]

Eisenhower was loath to spend the huge sums of money necessary for a nationwide shelter program even as policymakers in Washington considered the value of passive defense versus active defense. Delivered to President Eisenhower in November 1957, the Gaither Committee's report, *Deterrence and Survival in the Nuclear Age*, declared that by 1959, the United States would be extremely susceptible to a Soviet ICBM offensive, and it called for a $44-billion increase in defense spending over the next five years, which was "more than the entire defense budget for 1958. Half the money would go for more missiles and bombers…and half for a massive fallout shelter building program and other civil defense."[94]

Though fiscally conservative and wishing to avoid increased spending based on principle, Eisenhower also had another reason to avoid increased defense spending: the U-2 spy plane had provided the president proof that the Soviet Union was not increasing its nuclear arsenal or airplane fleet in preparation for war. Because it was a top-secret program used by the United States to spy on the Soviet Union, Eisenhower did not want to reveal this information or its source, though pressure on Eisenhower to catch up to the Soviet Union mounted. Eisenhower also wanted to avoid falsely giving the impression to the Soviet government that the United States was preparing for war by building fallout shelters, which could thereby increase the likelihood of war.[95]

However, widespread American fears of a Soviet nuclear attack spurred civil defense officials to prepare for its possibility by training Americans to respond through simulated bombings. This included Oklahoma participating "in a nationwide civil defense mock attack in May 1960," as reported by the *Altus Times-Democrat*; as a result "of the fictional hydrogen bomb attack, only 10 percent of Altus-area residents remained alive, and more casualties were expected among those survivors due to radiation exposure." The Altus newspaper also reported that a fictional nuclear bomb "hit near Martha." And, referring to one of the Atlas F ICBM sites then under construction near Altus Air Force Base, the newspaper also reported "another [hit] southwest of Altus near the missile site not yet built."[96]

President Kennedy appeared to view civil defense differently than President Eisenhower. In a May 25, 1961 special message to Congress, President Kennedy articulated his desire to strengthen the nation's civil defense and enhance the federal government's role in providing it:

> *One major element of the national security program which this Nation has never squarely faced up to is civil defense. In the past decade we have considered a variety of programs, but we have never adopted a consistent policy....*
>
> *This administration has been looking very hard at exactly what civil defense can and cannot do. It cannot be obtained cheaply. It cannot give an assurance of blast protection that will be proof against surprise attack or guarantee against obsolescence or destruction. And it cannot deter a nuclear attack.*
>
> *We will deter an enemy from making a nuclear attack only if our retaliatory power is so strong and so invulnerable that he knows he would be destroyed by our response....*
>
> *But this deterrent concept assumes rational calculations by rational men. And the history of this planet is sufficient to remind us of the possibilities of*

an irrational attack, a miscalculation, or an accidental war which cannot be either foreseen or deterred. The nature of modern warfare heightens these possibilities. It is on this basis that civil defense can readily be justified—as insurance for the civilian population in the event of such a miscalculation. It is insurance which we could never forgive ourselves for foregoing in the event of catastrophe.[97]

To fund his new civil defense initiative, Kennedy followed this message by sending a July supplemental appropriations request of $207.6 million to Congress, which virtually doubled the civil defense requests made during Eisenhower's presidency. Signaling its agreement with President Kennedy, Congress fully funded the request. The newly established Office of Civil Defense utilized the funds and initiated a nationwide survey to identify existing structures to be used as fallout shelters and to stock them with supplies.[98]

The August 1, 1961 edition of the *Altus Times-Democrat* carried a UPI story about Secretary of Defense Robert McNamara's appearance before Congress that day in which he reported that "perhaps several tens of millions" of Americans could be killed if the country were attacked with nuclear weapons. Under a directive from President Kennedy the same day, McNamara assumed control of national civil defense. He appeared before a House subcommittee taking up the issue to appeal for funding for President Kennedy's civil defense program to identify and mark "enough community shelter space in existing buildings" to accommodate fifty million Americans, which was approximately 25 percent of the country's population in 1962. McNamara used the hearing as an opportunity to criticize previous inaction by saying that President Kennedy was eager to "revitalize this long-neglected program."[99]

Fallout shelters were intended to protect citizens from nuclear fallout, radioactive dust from a nuclear explosion that can be blown miles downwind until falling back to earth. If the Soviet Union had attacked the United States with nuclear bombs, even Americans who avoided injury or death due to an explosion would have needed protection from drifting radioactive fallout until it decayed and no longer posed a threat. Shelters were intended to provide that protection.[100]

When President Kennedy embarked on a national fallout shelter program in light of the Berlin crisis in 1961, Stillwater had been on the forefront of civil defense preparedness for a decade. In 1951, Oklahoma A&M (as Oklahoma State University was then known) "was the very first school" in the nation "to teach Civil Defense courses. The school taught technical training in two-week courses" beginning July 30, 1951. "The Federal Civil Defense Administration (FCDA) gave quotas to Midwestern Civil Defense directors who assigned trainees to attend the school." This training "included health, welfare, rescue, police, fire fighting, and other services." The school was made available to the general public in 1952, and students could choose to attend the full two-week sessions or classes that met as few as five days and cost eighteen dollars. Though the FCDA closed it in August that year, the Oklahoma Civil Defense Agency reopened it. In 1957, the school began offering classes for women to learn "practical rescue work." The school's popularity increased throughout the decade and served approximately four thousand students by 1959.[101]

President Kennedy's 1961 call to the nation to find and provision fallout shelters—which would be marked with what became the familiar sign with three yellow triangles surrounded by a black circle—was answered by Stillwater's civil defense director, Bill Thomas. Survival supplies arrived in Stillwater in March 1963 for the shelters that Thomas and the Stillwater Civil Defense Agency surveyed and marked as meeting the government's criteria. "Water barrels, carbohydrate supplements, survival crackers, and sanitation kits rolled in to Stillwater for volunteers to store in their homes." Local preparedness efforts expanded as a "mobile hospital was stocked and staff prepared."[102]

To qualify as a public shelter, a space had to accommodate a minimum of fifty people, "include one cubic foot of storage space per person, and have a radiation protection factor of at least 100."[103] The Defense Supply Agency within the Department of Defense provided supplies to local governments, which assumed responsibility for stocking the shelters in their area. The Department of Defense created the federal fallout shelter sign in December 1961, and one was placed on each shelter that met the federal government's criteria.

The Office of Civil Defense created a handbook for citizens in January 1962 with instructions for building eight different kinds of home fallout shelters in basements or backyards to accommodate people who either lacked public shelter access or simply preferred shelter at home. The smallest would accommodate three people and cost less than $75 to build, and the largest would accommodate ten people and cost approximately $550 to build. Each shelter was intended to be built as inexpensively as possible, which meant that most of the shelters required the homeowner to perform the construction. The eight different shelters were the "Basement Sand-Filled

Lumber Lean-To Shelter," the "Basement Corrugated Asbestos-Cement Lean-To Shelter," the "Basement Concrete Block Shelter," the "Outside Semimounded Plywood Box Shelter," the "Belowground Corrugated Steel Culvert Shelter," the "Outside Semimounded Steel Igloo Shelter," the "Aboveground Earth-Covered Lumber A-Frame Shelter" and the "Belowground New Construction Clay Masonry Shelter." The last shelter was designed to be added to a new house under construction.[104]

Following the national pattern, Elk City in Beckham County formed a local civil defense contingent in December 1961, and this body included a twenty-three-man board. Elk City's civil defense unit included four directors in the 1960s: Welbourne Wood, Julius Pierce, Pat Patterson and Kirk Noakes. Though the Cold War was a dangerous time for all Americans, the danger was heightened for Elk City's residents because nearby Clinton-Sherman Air Force Base in Burns Flat was presumed to be a target if the Soviet Union attacked. The Washita County air force facility, fourteen miles southeast of Elk City, had been designated as a Strategic Air Command base, and it operated fifteen B-52 bombers. Those planes carried nuclear bombs and, according to protocols, "were in the air much of the time, flying to and from the Arctic Circle" in case offensive action against the Soviet Union was needed. "SAC strategy called for twelve armed B-52s to be in the air constantly, prepared to bomb the Soviet Union should war come."[105]

Concerned about regional civil defense preparedness, students and faculty at Southwestern Oklahoma State University (known as Southwestern State College in the 1960s) in Weatherford worked in tandem to educate the public about communications needs during a disaster. The February 6, 1962 edition of the student newspaper, the *Southwestern*, carried the story "Students Ready for Emergency," advertising ham radio operation classes on campus. The classes, taught by faculty members Grant Hendrix and Perry K. Jones with assistance from student ham operators Kenneth Bell and Bob Hill and student physics club president Richard Bates, would instruct participants in "elementary theory and code for amateur operators" and cost $2 per student. The story relates that ham radio operators would be vital if regular communications were disrupted during an emergency, and it emphasized their importance to the area's civil defense.[106]

The October 1962 Cuban missile crisis brought the world to the brink of nuclear war. State and local civil defense organizations prepared themselves for attack and encouraged the public to maintain vigilance during the crisis. Elk City's residents received the scare of their lives during this tense thirteen days due to a technical malfunction of the city's emergency alert sirens. The

SWOSU student ham radio operators Kenneth Bell *(left)* and Bob Hill appear in this photograph accompanying a civil defense story in the February 6, 1962 *Southwestern. Courtesy of the author.*

Thursday, October 25 edition of the *Elk City Daily News* referenced Herman Johnson, who oversaw the city's siren system, and explained to the city's residents that its emergency sirens sounded false alarms the previous Tuesday and Saturday in the midst of the crisis because of "an apparent short-circuit." Johnson said that Southwestern Bell's telephone specialists were brought in to fix the problem. He also explained that in an actual emergency, "the siren system will be blasted for 8 seconds then be off 4 seconds and then be repeated for a total of 3 minutes." The article relayed that the false alarm the previous day resulted in many parents simultaneously rushing to schools to collect their children and creating "near panic conditions."[107]

The same edition of the Elk City newspaper carried a UPI story about increased state civil defense activity during the crisis. Oklahoma civil defense director Jerry Ragsdale even released a statement "to 355 local directors" in which he said, "We urge that you update and review your local disaster plans as soon as possible and make them current so as to coincide with present world conditions." Built to provide protection from a bomb blast and nuclear fallout, the bomb shelter under the capitol building in Oklahoma City, on track to be completed in just over a month, would be used as state government headquarters if necessitated by an attack. Public shelters were also available at several locations on the capitol grounds, including the cafeteria and areas inside the capitol building itself. According to the story, "between 800 and 1,000 public buildings in the state" were available as public shelters, and public shelters in Oklahoma City were scheduled to receive emergency supplies beginning that night. The story also relayed that civil defense sirens in Sand Springs would be tested each day for the duration of the Cuban crisis.[108]

The Friday, October 26, 1962 edition of the *Elk City Daily News* reported that the city's civil defense committee met that morning to establish "certain rules for the protection of local citizens in the event of an enemy attack" and to announce that the city's warning sirens would be tested the following Tuesday evening. Committee chairman Welbourne Wood also announced that, in the event of an attack during the school day, children would remain at school until their parents collected them unless parents had granted written permission for their children to leave. However, in an apparent attempt to avoid chaos among panicked parents frantically fetching their children at those schools, the newspaper relayed Wood's suggestion that a school building was "perhaps one of the safest places for children to be in the event of a nuclear attack."[109] The same story announced that the basements of the city's Baptist church building and the Casa Grande Hotel had been approved by the U.S. Corps of Engineers as the city's two public fallout shelters. A third shelter was being planned, and its location would eventually be made known to the public. Wood reminded the public that these shelters were intended for people who were away from home during an attack, and he encouraged families to prepare their homes as shelters to avoid overcrowding the public shelters. Wood conveyed that families should do the following in the event of an alarm: "1. Draw as much water as possible. 2. Find shelter in or near the home and then stay there. 3. Be sure to have a small stock of canned goods…enugh [*sic*] for one or two days. 4. Have on hand medical supplies. 5. After an alarm has sounded, do not look in the direction of Clinton-Sherman air base." The article ended with Wood's hope that these preparations would help Elk City's residents survive a nuclear weapons attack.[110]

City, county and air force civil defense officials in Jackson County also coordinated efforts during the Cuban missile crisis. The October 23, 1962 edition of the *Altus Times-Democrat* featured a front-page story about a meeting between Altus Air Force Base civil defense director Lieutenant Colonel Richard Maffry, Jackson County civil defense director Tal Oden, Altus civil defense director Rex Bailey and Frank Wimberly, general manager of KWHW Radio. The story relayed that Oden encouraged Jackson County residents to prepare for a possible nuclear attack and provide shelter for family and even employees. Oden said that local media would inform the public with updates about international tensions, and Altus residents would be warned of an attack through the city's emergency sirens. Oden "said a warning is two 3-minute blasts on the local siren and this indicates all citizens should inform themselves by radio and-or TV of the existing situation." He also said that if an attack was imminent, "the siren will wail continuously, warning the citizens to take the best shelter available immediately." He encouraged the public to stock shelters with adequate food, water and medical supplies while also encouraging citizens to avoid "excess anxiety" that "might result in hampering effective and prompt survival action." Oden went on to remind the public in Altus that KWHW Radio was "under a 24-hour alerting system through joint responsibility of the Defense Department and the United Press International." In light of this, the radio station would quickly provide the public with "alert information."[111]

In the immediate aftermath of the Cuban missile crisis, the SWOSU student newspaper announced that civil defense radioactivity monitoring classes—begun the previous spring "in cooperation with the state and national civil defense authority"—would continue. The October 30, 1962 edition of the *Southwestern* explained the classes, which would be "[o]f interest to Southwestern…students…in light of the recent developments in Cuba," would continue to be taught by campus chemistry professor Dr. Donald Hamm. The two-dollar enrollment fee would cover all costs, and students would receive instruction in using Geiger counters. The program was intended "to instruct college students and individuals in the southwest area of the state concerning the action and dangers of radioactivity and methods of detecting and measuring it."[112]

Located in northwest Washita County, Canute is eight miles east of Elk City. As tensions continued to relax after the Cuban missile crisis, the November 4, 1962 *Elk City Daily News* announced that family survival courses would begin the next day at the Canute High School building "for all area families interested in learning how to survive a nuclear attack," according to Canute schools superintendent A.D. Castle. The twelve-hour course, "sponsored by the U.S. Office of Education," was divided into four separate nights throughout November. In addition to teaching strategies to survive a nuclear war, the classes were advertised as addressing "the nature of modern weapons of war, their effects and the civil defense effort." Another goal of the class was to create informed local civil defense leadership groups.[113]

Elk City added more fallout shelters in the 1960s. In addition to the Casa Grande Hotel and the First Baptist Church building, a fallout shelter was designated in the basement of Community Hospital. In 1966, the city built a basement shelter behind the facility that housed both the police station and fire station. The shelters were stocked with provisions to last occupants two weeks. Additionally, Elk City "had sixteen civil defense monitoring stations that would send information concerning radioactive fallout conditions, and each station had two or three trained monitors. Stan Young was the radiological monitoring officer of the city's civil defense unit."[114]

The water drums provided by the federal government for local community shelters held 17.5 gallons of water. Each drum was intended to provide five people one quart of water a day for up to two weeks. Drums were made of fiberboard or, later, steel, included two plastic liners and "stood about 22 inches tall and…about 16 inches in diameter."[115] One liner held water, and the other liner was an extra to be used if needed. When filled with water, the polyethylene liners were either sealed with heat or tied. In normal conditions, the metal drums and polyethylene liners were expected to have a storage life of more than ten years.

The Office of Civil Defense issued food guidelines in June 1964 for federally stocked fallout shelters. Though 1,500 calories per day was determined sufficient to sustain daily activity for an individual, the government believed "that healthy persons can subsist for periods up to the maximum anticipated confinement of 2 weeks under sedentary conditions on a survival ration of 700 calories per day." The government considered seven requirements in determining appropriate fallout shelter foods: "the food be palatable or at least acceptable to the majority of the shelter occupants; have sufficient storage stability to permit a shelf life of 5 to 10 years; be obtainable at low cost; be widely available or easily produced; have high bulk density to conserve storage space; require little or no preparation; and produce a minimum trash volume."[116] In light of these criteria, the Armed Forces Food and Container Institute chose four items with which to stock shelters: survival biscuits, survival crackers, carbohydrate supplements and bulgur wafers. They were packaged separately in sealed cans with an estimated shelf life of between five and fifteen years.

In addition to food and water, the federal government also stocked each community shelter with a medical kit. Initially developed in the 1962 fiscal year and slightly altered after the 1966 fiscal year, it was provided for physical ailments, including emergencies, as well as for "controlling emotional stress." The supplies fell into three categories: "medication," "dressings" and "other." The medication included aspirin, Eugenol, eye and nose drops, isopropyl alcohol, kaolin and pectin mixture, penicillin, petrolatum, phenobarbital, surgical soap, sodium bicarbonate, sodium chloride and sulfadiazine. The dressings included bandages, gauze, muslin, purified cotton and surgical pads. "Other" items included cotton-tipped applicators, tongue depressors, forceps, safety pins, scissors, thermometers and an instruction manual. The general storage life in normal conditions for the items was estimated at a minimum of five years and a maximum of at least ten years, with all of the dressings and most of the "other" items listed as having an indefinite storage life.[117]

In 1964, six hundred thousand fallout shelters had been marked in Oklahoma. Some of these were designated at several buildings on the SWOSU campus in Weatherford. The October 13, 1964 *Southwestern* carried a story announcing that "eight approved and fully stocked fallout shelters" were available if needed. "Food and first aid supplies" for the shelters had arrived the previous week and had been delivered to the basement in each building. According to Southwestern dean of students and civil defense director W.C. Burris, the shelter provisions cost $4,168.43 and would supply "2,062 persons during a period of two weeks."[118]

Southwestern speech and philosophy professor Dr. James Sill was featured in the December 8, 1964 *Southwestern* because he was digging by hand a dual-purpose storm and fallout shelter at his home at 1212 North Caddo Street in Weatherford. The story's writer prefaced his piece about the defense-minded professor with information that gives insight into what supplies each campus shelter included: "Campus basements are loaded down with food stuffs, huge water containers, radiation detectors, and first aid kits courtesy of the federal government's fall-out shelter program." In addition to being a professor, Sill was also "a lieutenant colonel in the Army reserves" and thought that the project was an excellent opportunity for him to get exercise.[119] The story also conveyed that as campus civil defense director, Dean Burris equipped the eight campus fallout shelters "in the basements of Stewart, Neff and Quannah Parker dormitories, as well as in the student center, old science, education and new science buildings." The story reiterated that the shelters could hold approximately two thousand students, and Burris emphasized the need for the college to be prepared for an attack because of its location. "Looking at a state map, we see that we are in a rather strategic position. Southwestern is surrounded by military installations at Tinker, Clinton-Sherman, Altus and Lawton."[120]

Basil Weatherly was an Elk City High School sophomore when public fallout shelters were first designated there in 1966. A conscientious, civic-minded teenager who was also captivated by the American space program, Weatherly and several other local high school students formed a civil defense support group to aid the adult civil defense unit responsible for guiding the city through a nuclear attack. According to Weatherly in a June 2018 interview and an undated story from the *Elk City Daily News* pasted in his scrapbook that he showed the author, the Elk City civil defense support group he was a member of was the first of its kind in Oklahoma.[121] I.A. Patterson was Elk City's civil defense director then, and local pharmacist Kirk Noakes was the assistant director. The high school civil defense support group met each week for classes taught by Noakes in the fallout shelter, which also served as the emergency operations center behind the building that housed the police station and fire department. "We discussed various nuclear attack scenarios and how to respond," Weatherly said. Classes were also attended by the mayor, police chief, fire chief, city manager and civil defense director.[122] Each member of the support group was issued a yellow jumpsuit with the words "Civil Defense Rescue Elk City, Okla" stitched on the back. Each member was also issued a dosimeter to detect radiation after a nuclear blast. If a nuclear attack was believed to be imminent, the group was instructed to report to the emergency operations center.[123]

Another undated story from the *Elk City Daily News* in Weatherly's scrapbook shows that the Elk City civil defense group attended an instructional meeting in nearby Sayre, county seat of Beckham County. "Observing a disaster training conducted Tuesday at the Sayre hospital were I.A. Patterson, Elk City's civil defense director, Danny Storm, Richard Heine and Basil Weatherly, members of Elk City's support team, and Mr. and Mrs. Kirk Noakes and John Owens." According to the story, the training was in conjunction with the Oklahoma Health Department.[124]

As Weatherly reminisced and spoke of his memories with the civil defense support group in the mid- to late 1960s, he reflected on the concern he, his friends and other locals had for their safety. "It was still looking pretty grim then," Weatherly said. His concern, and a desire to help, motivated him and others—even though they were just teenagers. "We realized what we could contribute at the local level," Weatherly said. Of course, he was still a teenager who was motivated by more than just civic duty. Speaking of the chance to be part of Elk City's civil defense support group, Weatherly

Right: Stewart Hall, a ladies' dorm, was one of eight fallout shelters on the SWOSU campus in Weatherford. This photograph from the 1966 SWOSU yearbook shows a fallout shelter sign below and to the left of the "Stewart Hall" sign. *Courtesy of the author.*

Below: Neff Hall, a gentlemen's dorm that was one of the designated fallout shelters on the SWOSU campus in Weatherford, as it appears today. *Courtesy of the author.*

Above: The Old Science Building was one of the designated fallout shelters on the SWOSU campus in Weatherford. This photograph of musicians performing on the south steps of Old Science was included in the 1970 SWOSU yearbook. A fallout shelter sign is visible in the upper left. *Courtesy of the author.*

Left: Undated *Elk City Daily News* photograph from Elk City resident Basil Weatherly's scrapbook. *Courtesy of the author.*

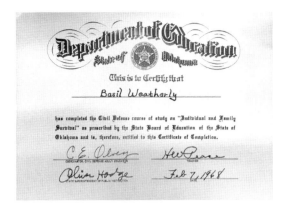

Basil Weatherly's Oklahoma Department of Education certification of completion for an "Individual and Family Survival" course, dated February 7, 1968. *Courtesy of the author.*

admitted that he had a lot of fun: "I relished the opportunity," he said. "It was exciting. It was cool."[125]

The teenage civil defense group was not limited to just preparing for a nuclear attack. They also helped storm spotters track the sometimes violent western Oklahoma spring thunderstorms. A May 8, 1968 story from the *Elk City Daily News* pasted into Weatherly's scrapbook reports: "Members of the local high school civil defense support team were busy charting the path of the storm that hit the Erick area Monday night." An accompanying photograph shows group secretary Gary Barnes, captain Randy Haggard, cocaptain Ted Anderson and liaison officer Basil Weatherly, then an eighteen-year-old senior on the verge of graduating from Elk City High School.[126]

After graduating in 1968, Weatherly left Elk City and went to college in nearby Weatherford. He said that as the 1960s became the 1970s and tensions between the United States and the Soviet Union diminished—along with the threat of a nuclear war—the need for the civil defense support team also diminished. The group disbanded sometime in the 1970s.[127]

When President Kennedy was assassinated in November 1963, space for 110 million shelters had been identified around the nation, of which 70 million were available for use and 14 million were stocked with supplies. However, the first year of Lyndon Johnson's presidency, Congress appropriated only $105.2 million of the Office of Civil Defense's requested $358 million. By 1968, the final year of Johnson's presidency, the amount requested fell to $77.3 million, of which Congress appropriated only $60.5 million. According to Wayne Blanchard, the lack of support for civil defense from President Johnson and Secretary McNamara—caused by the acceptance of the philosophy of mutual assured destruction, the fear that civil defense

From the May 8, 1968 *Elk City Daily* News. The Elk City High School civil defense support team member at the far left is eighteen-year-old Basil Weatherly. *Courtesy of the author.*

preparations would actually trigger nuclear war and the prohibitive costs of the Vietnam War—influenced Congress to withhold support as well.[128]

A 1964 SWOSU graduate, Bob Klaassen went to work for his alma mater in 1978 and retired from the university as its registrar in 2010. In a 2018 interview, Klaassen reminisced about his time occupying an office in a building where civil defense supplies were still stored in what had served as one of the campus's fallout shelters. "I have memories of large barrels of water in the basement of the Administration Building," Klaassen said. He also said that after the Cold War ended, the small civil defense fallout shelter signs that had adorned several campus buildings "were removed without any fanfare."[129]

The threat of an attack led to the development of the federal emergency Thunderbolt siren for civil defense in the early 1950s. The design is distinctive, as is its method of operation. Air from a pump is forced through the rotor, called the chopper, and the siren, usually mounted atop a tall pole, emits sound "at full volume throughout the chopper pitch range."[130] Elk City installed several yellow Thunderbolt sirens during the Cold War for nuclear attack warning, but the sirens were also used to warn of severe weather. Elk City's Thunderbolt sirens, like the one currently mounted atop a wooden power pole behind the Elk City Fire Department, are used solely as storm sirens today, warning residents of an imminent tornado instead of an imminent nuclear missile attack.

Elk City's current fire chief and emergency management director, Billy Word, joined the Elk City Fire Department in February 1989, nine months before the fall of the Berlin Wall—the beginning of the Cold War's end. Today, the civil defense supplies that once stocked the fallout shelter in the Elk City Fire Department basement sit in an unassuming metal storage building at Elk City Municipal Airport. Though he cannot say with certainty, Word believes that those supplies were likely moved there in the mid- to late 1990s, after the Soviet Union disintegrated in 1991 and the Cold War ended.[131] Like the removal of fallout shelter supplies and signs at SWOSU in Weatherford, the inability to pinpoint when the Elk City supplies were taken to storage speaks to the unceremonious fashion in which the Cold War ended in the United States, and years'

Elk City Fire Department as it appears today. The building was one of Elk City's designated public fallout shelters. *Courtesy of the author.*

Thunderbolt civil defense siren behind the Elk City Fire Department. *Courtesy of the author.*

Civil defense storage building at Elk City Municipal Airport, June 2018. *Courtesy of the author.*

Top: Civil defense supplies in storage at Elk City Municipal Airport. *Courtesy of the author.*

Middle: Federal sanitation kit in civil defense storage at Elk City Municipal Airport. *Courtesy of the author.*

Bottom: Radiological survey meter and dosimeters in civil defense storage at Elk City Municipal Airport. *Courtesy of the author.*

Federal 17.5-gallon water drum in civil defense storage at Elk City Municipal Airport. *Courtesy of the author.*

worth of planning and preparation for life-threatening nuclear attack became a distant memory for Americans, more difficult to recall with each passing day.

The manner in which fallout shelter signs and supplies were removed in Elk City and Weatherford was emblematic of how the forty-five-year conflict called the Cold War ended in the early 1990s—with a whimper instead of a bang. This belied the danger, fear and, at times, panic that gripped Oklahomans during the early 1960s as the Cold War entered its most dangerous period, punctuated by the hair-raising Cuban missile crisis of October 1962. The Cold War ethos of civil defense preparedness became part of Oklahoma's "new normal" as the state's communities and college campuses joined national civilian preparedness efforts to survive a nuclear attack during the Cold War's hottest and most frightening years.

7

CHILDHOOD MEMORIES, DISCOVERY AND STALE CRACKERS

orn in 1976, I was a child of the 1980s. Every Friday night at home in Elk City, my family and I watched Bo and Luke Duke burn up the dirt roads of Hazzard County, Georgia, fleeing the hot pursuit of Sheriff Roscoe P. Coltrane on *The Dukes of Hazzard*. Afterward, we stayed glued to the television to enjoy the Texas-style cowboy villainy of oil tycoon J.R. Ewing on *Dallas*.

The first U.S. presidency I remember was that of Ronald Reagan, and though I remember hearing the names Andropov and Chernenko as a child, the first leader of the Soviet Union I remember seeing on television was Reagan's Cold War adversary—then partner in peace—Mikhail Gorbachev.

Looking back, every fourth movie must have been a Cold War drama about conflict with the Soviet Union—*Iron Eagle, Rocky IV, Top Gun. Red Dawn* scared me. Thankfully, I never watched *The Day After*.

I remember being vaguely aware of something called "nuclear war" in the 1980s, and I remember being afraid of it.

One bright, sunny day when I was eight or nine, in 1984 or 1985, storm sirens sounded in Elk City, and our babysitter grabbed my twin brother and me and we headed outside. She glanced at the sky with a confused look on her face. Memories being vague and elusive, I don't remember what happened next. Looking back, I don't know if she suspected a tornado or a nuclear attack, but I remember that I was afraid.

I remember hearing the occasional Emergency Alert System test on the radio and on television. Each time I heard the distinctive sound on either,

Thunderbolt civil defense siren behind the Elk City Fire Department. *Courtesy of the author.*

I wondered if this would be an actual emergency. The recorded voice said that in an actual emergency we would be given instructions, though I don't know what those instructions would have been.

After speaking at the Stafford Air & Space Museum in Weatherford about the missiles of Oklahoma one February Friday night in 2018, I chatted with museum director Max Ary. We were talking about the Cuban missile crisis, and Max said that he vividly remembered it. He was in his early teens, and he watched news coverage of the crisis from a hospital bed where he was recuperating from a health issue. Max told me that he remembered thinking that nuclear war was imminent and that he would soon die because of it.

I don't have a Cold War memory that scary. In fact, the Cold War was winding down as I approached my teens. However, having lived through its final decade and a half and having studied and taught the Cold War as an adult, I have a sense of the fear that others who grew up in the 1950s, 1960s and 1970s felt. Until writing this part of this book, though, I didn't know who was involved in Cold War civil defense preparedness in Elk City, Weatherford and western Oklahoma. In fact, I was unaware of the extent of civil defense preparations here. I didn't know that an Elk City emergency siren malfunctioned during the Cuban missile crisis, creating extreme fear among parents whose children were at school. As a parent, I can imagine that fear.

I didn't know that public buildings in Elk City were designated as public fallout shelters and stocked with food, water and medical supplies. I owe a huge thank-you to Elk City fire chief Billy Word. He patiently answered my questions about civil defense sirens, fallout shelters and food, equipment and medical supplies that they contained. He showed me the underground shelter that served as Elk City's emergency operations center. He also volunteered to show me the unassuming metal storage building at Elk City Municipal Airport that houses what remains of Elk City's civil defense fallout shelter supplies. He's the reason that pictures of those supplies and equipment are included in this book. Thanks, Chief.

I didn't know that Elk City High School students formed a civil defense support group in the 1960s, let alone the state's first. I owe a debt of gratitude to Elk City's Basil Weatherly for sharing his memories of his part in the Elk City civil defense support group and for sharing his scrapbook. Thanks, Basil.

I was seven in 1982, and I didn't know that relocation plans had been made in the state in case of nuclear attack. David Van Nostrand was civil defense program director for Edmond, Oklahoma, then. He reflected on his childhood memories of civil defense drills when he and classmates were told to "get down and cover our heads" in the "duck-and-cover position." He also recalled educational films and television programs that said to look away from the bright light of an explosion. By the early 1980s, the approach to nuclear survival had changed. The renewed arms race also renewed worry about nuclear war and the need for civil defense. In those days, though, "crisis relocation" had become the primary means of surviving a nuclear attack. Described as a "head-for-the-hills plan" by the *Daily Oklahoman*, "380 U.S. cities and 90 other high-risk areas would be evacuated if nuclear war seemed imminent." According to the Department of Defense, the evacuation would take between three days and a week, but time would be available because "a period of international tension would precede any nuclear exchange."[132]

In 1982, seven Oklahoma locations were believed to be targeted by Soviet missiles: Tulsa because of its size and Oklahoma City, McAlester, Lawton, Altus, Burns Flat and Enid because they were close to military facilities. The plan called for residents of those places to relocate to "host communities" in other counties. A government-produced booklet encouraged "evacuees to take a three-day supply of food" and "about 50 other items including gloves, a flashlight, soap and an emergency toilet." People would be pointed toward fallout shelters.[133]

A crisis relocation pilot program was undertaken by eight U.S. cities in the mid-1970s, and Oklahoma City was one of them. By 1982, Oklahoma's evacuation plan was considered nearly complete. By the early 1980s, the Federal Emergency Management Agency oversaw the country's civil defense, and it argued that these crisis relocation plans "could save 80 percent of the population in the event of a nuclear attack."[134]

I learned that Oklahoma City's evacuation plan would send its residents in different directions. People "living in northwest Oklahoma City could be directed to Custer County, while those living in the southeast sector of the city could be headed to Pontotoc County." According to Lee Akin, deputy director of Oklahoma's state civil defense agency in 1982, once the evacuation plan would go into effect, residents could go anywhere they chose for shelter during an eight-hour "free period." "Those who don't want to leave at all 'will just be shoved aside to make room for those who do want to go,'" Akin said.[135]

A 1978 Central Intelligence Agency report stated that the nation would have a week to prepare for evacuation before a Soviet nuclear attack. This was based on a belief that the Soviet Union planned to also evacuate its major cities prior to launching a nuclear strike against the United States. This belief was based on the presumed Soviet goal "of leaving itself 'in a stronger postwar position than its adversaries.' "[136]

Again, I'm glad that, as a child, I was unaware of these plans.

I learned that late in the 1980s, when heightened fears were subsiding as the Cold War was beginning to wind down, the state had to figure out what to do with its aging food that had been stockpiled in fallout shelters. In July 1988, Oklahoma City's council announced that "350 tons of rancid Civil Defense survival crackers" were surplus, and it was grappling with how to dispose of them. Having been "manufactured by the Keebler Co. between July and December 1962," by 1988, the crackers had been stored in Oklahoma City fallout shelters for twenty-six years. J.J. Steward was director of civil defense, then called emergency management, and he was not eager to jettison the food, saying, "A stale cracker would still taste better than a grubworm or a rat."[137]

I wish I *had* known that.

Though I'm a SWOSU graduate and a member of the SWOSU social sciences faculty, I didn't know that several buildings on the SWOSU campus

The only remaining exterior fallout shelter sign on the SWOSU campus in Weatherford, June 2018. *Courtesy of the author.*

in Weatherford were designated as fallout shelters and were stocked in the 1960s. SWOSU provost Dr. James South helped me locate the remaining fallout shelter signs on the SWOSU campus in Weatherford. Thanks, James.

Interestingly, nobody knows why those two SWOSU Administration Building fallout shelter signs—one outside, one inside—remain while all of the others have, apparently, been removed. I'm just glad that they remain as reminders of our past.

Before writing this book, I didn't know that a SWOSU professor dug a fallout shelter by hand. Come to think of it, I didn't know that anyone had dug a fallout shelter by hand, or that SWOSU offered civil defense–related classes in the 1960s. I've learned so much, for which I'm so thankful.

Elk City, Weatherford, Altus and several other Oklahoma cities joined thousands of others around the nation in preparing for a nuclear attack. Oklahoma communities played a vital offensive role in building missile sites and housing intercontinental ballistic missiles that were part of the American nuclear arsenal in the 1960s. Many more communities throughout the state implemented civil defense measures to survive a Soviet nuclear attack that, at times, seemed imminent.

Oklahoma communities mounted vigorous offense and defense during the Cold War's most dangerous years. Both are worth learning about. I'm glad that I did.

8

OKLAHOMA MILITARY INSTALLATIONS

As happened elsewhere in the country, Oklahoma saw the rise and expansion of military installations as World War II gave way to the Cold War. Oklahoma communities were impacted as thousands of military personnel and civilians arrived in the state to play their part in serving this country. Tinker Air Force Base, Vance Air Force Base, Clinton-Sherman Air Force Base, the U.S. Army Ammunition Plant, Fort Sill and Altus Air Force Base played important roles in training troops to fight around the world against declared enemies and to defend the nation against conventional or nuclear attack.

TINKER AIR FORCE BASE

Named for Pawhuska native Major General Clarence L. Tinker, Tinker Air Force Base in Oklahoma City began as a maintenance and supply depot before American involvement in World War II. The War Department formally awarded the depot on April 8, 1941. "During World War II, Tinker's industrial plant repaired B-24 and B-17 bombers and fitted B-29s for combat."[138] Tinker was active maintaining America's warplanes during the first Cold War conflict the country fought, the 1950–53 Korean War. The base also maintained important roles in the 1956 Suez crisis, the 1961 Berlin crisis and the 1962 Cuban missile crisis. Then, in the Vietnam War,

"Tinker provided logistics and communications support to Air Force units in Southeast Asia."[139]

The base has had multiple brushes with fame. Early in 1946, personnel "began modifying B-29s for atomic testing near the Bikini Atoll, and the historic *Enola Gay* made its first visit to Tinker for an overhaul." The next year, President Truman's airplane, a C-54 called the "Sacred Cow," was modified there. A large tornado in March 1948 damaged the base and aircraft at a cost of more than $10 million. Just five days later, another tornado threat loomed. "On March 25, 1948, base meteorologists issued the first official tornado warning in American history." Months later, when Soviet leader Joseph Stalin blockaded the German capital of Berlin in an effort to force the Americans out of the western portion of the city, Tinker personnel traveled to England to help implement the nuts and bolts of the Berlin Airlift, which overcame the blockade.[140]

The KC-135 Stratotanker is the largest version of the Boeing C-135 aircraft and is used to refuel other planes while in the air. Tinker Air Force Base maintains the Stratotanker. "The C-135/KC-135 aircraft was first produced in 1955 and has served in every major conflict and many other missions around the world for the U.S. Air Force."[141] Cold War service included refueling bombers for Strategic Air Command and fighters for Tactical Air Command.

Boeing first partnered with Tinker Air Force Base in the early 1950s, when the base provided maintenance for the B-29 and B-47 bombers and then began readying itself to be depot for the B-52 bomber in 1953. In the 1980s, the B-1 bomber program reappeared at Tinker, and Boeing's presence at the base intensified. The Airborne Warning and Control System, or AWACS—the Boeing E-3 Sentry—has been in service for more than forty years and is operated at Tinker. This workhorse "has supported every major U.S. military operation from the Cold War to the global war on terror."[142]

The enormous B-52 was built to carry nuclear bombs to the Soviet Union, but today it "is capable of dropping or launching the widest array of weapons in the U.S. inventory, everything from cluster bombs to cruise missiles," according to Adam Kemp. Several of the modifications necessary for this to happen were made at Tinker. Fear of nuclear war in the early Cold War was reflected in the B-52's constant nuclear readiness, when a dozen "were constantly airborne with a full payload of nuclear weapons as part of Operation Chrome Dome." Because each could carry fifty thousand gallons of fuel and be refueled in flight, "crews flew 24-hour missions. Each flight path resulted in a B-52 never being more than two-hours flying time from an enemy target, waiting for the 'go codes' that would alert them to drop their devastating weapons." In Vietnam, the plane's mission changed, and it began supporting operations on the ground. Far fewer B-52s still fly, but those that do are serviced at Tinker Air Force Base.[143]

One of the most colorful weapons to pass through Tinker was the AGM-28 Hound Dog missile. This large missile, named for the Elvis Presley song, was carried by the B-52 Stratofortress bomber, one under each wing. Greg L. Davis writes that, as Cold War tensions rose in 1956, the U.S. Air Force requested "an air-to-surface missile to give the B-52 extended stand-off capability." Special pylons to attach the Hound Dogs to the planes "were installed in two work surges at Tinker beginning on Feb. 14, 1960." Each Hound Dog missile had an engine that propelled it, carried a four-megaton nuclear warhead—approximately the same strength as the nuclear warhead on the Atlas F missiles and more than two hundred times more powerful than the atomic bombs dropped on Hiroshima and Nagasaki—and had a seven-hundred-mile range, allowing the B-52 that carried it to avoid target and explosion proximity. The missile would be launched at 45,000 feet, "climb to...60,000 feet and then dive to impact the target from above." At 42.5 feet long, more than 12 feet wide, more than 9 feet tall and weighing more than 10,100 pounds when operational, the Hound Dog was "the largest American air-to-surface missile ever built." It was never used in combat.[144]

VANCE AIR FORCE BASE

Located in north-central Oklahoma in the Garfield County city of Enid, Vance Air Force Base is named in honor of hometown World War II Congressional Medal of Honor recipient Lieutenant Colonel Leon R. "Bob" Vance Jr. The city was granted the base on June 19, 1941. First called the Air Corps Basic Flying School, in 1942 it became Enid Army Flying School, and then its name was changed again in 1943 to Enid Army Air Field. When World War II ended, so did the need for pilots, and the installation was deactivated in January 1947. If not for Floyd E. Welsh, it likely would have closed permanently. Assigned to the office of War Surplus Property—which was responsible for shuttering unnecessary bases—in the Pentagon, Major Welsh, an Alva, Oklahoma native, came across Enid Army Air Field's file in his stack of bases facing closure. He promptly put the file on the bottom of the stack. "When the Air Force decided to reopen several pilot training bases,

Welsh pulled out the Enid Army Flying Field file and passed it along to his superiors with a recommendation to reopen the base."[145] It was reopened as Enid Air Force Base in January 1948, and it was renamed Vance Air Force Base in July 1949.[146]

Vance began training pilot instructors ahead of the June 1950 commencement of the Korean War, when pilot demand increased, and "basic pilot training was added to the base mission," according to Thomas Hedglen. Several planes were available for base training, including the North American T-28 Trojan, the AT-6 Texan, the TB-25 and the T-33A Shooting Star. "In 1957, Vance became an all-jet training facility." Notables who touched down at Vance Air Force Base included Major Merlyn H. Dethlefsen, a base instructor in the waning years of the 1960s and winner of the Congressional Medal of Honor for his service in the Vietnam War. President Nixon also visited the base in 1974. The base saw the arrival of the first female pilot trainees in 1978, one of whom was Eileen M. Collins— the first female space shuttle commander for the National Aeronautics and Space Administration (NASA). Then, in 1982, "A two-day Astronaut Candidate Training Program began at Vance." Two of the participants in the program were astronauts Sally Ride and Kalpana Chawla.[147]

Clinton-Sherman Air Force Base

Clinton-Sherman Air Force Base was another World War II creation, christened Clinton Naval Air Station when it opened in October 1943. Located seventeen miles west-southwest of the Custer County city of Clinton, the base is actually situated in the city of Burns Flat in Washita County. The War Department laid claim to "five thousand acres of Washita County farmland…for a naval air station." Runways, hangars, barracks and other facilities were created. "More than thirty-five hundred officers and enlisted men" followed who "served with the Special Task Air Groups in the operation of aircraft drones and glider bombs."[148]

The naval air station closed after World War II, and the War Assets Administration transferred ownership to the City of Clinton. In September 1954, the federal government "leased the site from the city of Clinton and began extending one runway that eventually reached a length of 13,502 feet, constructing new facilities, and building nine hundred military family housing units." Renamed Clinton-Sherman Air Force Base, the new SAC base was devoted to training pilots and developing aircraft equipment. Over the next decade, the air force laid hold to several more acres of property.[149]

As the 1950s became the 1960s, Cold War commitments dictated the role of Clinton-Sherman Air Force Base. "In March 1959, with a new assignment of B-52s, the 4123d Strategic Wing and its Ninety-eighth Bombardment squadron arrived at Clinton-Sherman to conduct a nine-month test of the SAC airborne alert program." More changes began in early 1963. "The Seventieth Bombardment Wing, along with its Sixth Bombardment Squadron and 902d Air Refueling Squadron replaced the 4123d on February 1, 1963." The newly christened units underwent "strategic bombardment training and air refueling" with B-52s and KC-135s "to meet air force global commitments." Then, late in the decade, most aircrew and maintenance personnel spent time with various SAC units for combat "in the Far East and Southeast Asia." This proved to be a prelude to the base closing at the end of 1969. At more than 13,500 feet, its runway was at one time considered a possible landing location for NASA's space shuttle program, and the base has been used by personnel from Altus and Vance Air Force Bases for training purposes.[150]

Locals in and near Clinton-Sherman had heard since December 1965 that the base would likely close within a matter of four years as the Department of Defense looked to downsize its number of bases. "We were completely blindsided," Frank Kliewer, former Cordell businessman and Base Area Civilian Advisory Committee chairman, was quoted as saying in a 2005 *NewsOK* story. "We went to Washington several times after that, trying to stop the closure…but it didn't work."[151]

The base closure affected Burns Flat and several nearby communities. More than 3,000 people were employed by Clinton-Sherman Air Force Base, including 298 civilians. This translated into $14.4 million in annual wages lost, which negatively impacted area businesses. The $2.2 million for groceries, $2.25 million on housing, $2 million on automobiles, $1 million for furniture and nearly that much for clothes and entertainment spent annually was lost. All of this was felt in Elk City, where 1,156 residents were affiliated with the base; Cordell, where 865 were; and Clinton, where 709 residents were connected to Clinton-Sherman Air Force Base.[152]

The schools in those communities also lost students and related school aid each year to the tune of $390,000. Understandably, Burns Flat was hit hardest. The Burns Flat school system was Washita County's largest in 1965. That changed when the base closed. Former Burns Flat teacher Garline Thomas taught her first semester there in the fall of 1969. "When we returned from Christmas break our enrollment had dropped from some 1,700 students to 250 kids. I suddenly had my own classroom, but I had two, three, and sometimes six kids in a class."[153]

U.S. Army Ammunition Plant

Located in McAlester in Pittsburg County in southeast Oklahoma, the U.S. Army Ammunition Plant began as the U.S. Naval Ammunition Depot. As the nation prepared for war in the early 1940s, the War Department considered the need for inland ammunition depots. While the U.S. Army was uninterested in McAlester, the U.S. Navy showed a keen interest. "McAlester was an ideal location; it was far enough inland and lay at the intersections of major highways and railroads. The large land area southwest of the city was of fairly low quality and was sparsely populated, so acquisition of the area would cause few problems."[154] The navy announced that McAlester would be the location of a new depot on June 10, 1942.

By 1945, the plant employed "more than eight thousand." After World War II, those numbers dropped significantly, then they rose to three thousand during the Korean War. The number employed dropped again after the war, reaching six hundred by the end of the 1950s. However, war in Vietnam necessitated a more robust workforce, and another three thousand were hired. Then, "[o]n October 1, 1977, the depot became the U.S. Army Ammunition Plant, as a result of the Department of Defense's decision to place the army in charge of conventional ammunition for all the armed forces in order to increase efficiency."[155]

Fort Sill

Fort Sill, located near Lawton in Comanche County, began as a cavalry post in the late 1860s. In 1869, only four years after the Civil War's end, Fort Still was built. It was named by Major General Philip H. Sheridan for West Point classmate Brigadier General Joshua W. Sill, who was killed during the 1862 battle of Stones River in Tennessee. The cavalry units left, but by 1905, they were replaced by artillery regiments. Fort Sill housed the Field Artillery School by 1919 and came to permanently house field artillery.

In 1934, the Field Artillery Museum was created. Today it is known as the Fort Sill Museum.[156]

Fort Sill expanded during World War II and began training for the Forty-Fifth Infantry Division. "The U.S. Army Aviation School was added in 1945, and the following year the U.S. Army Artillery Center was established to test new equipment and doctrine."[157] The Fort Sill center combined that location's "Artillery School, the Antiaircraft and Guided Missile School at Fort Bliss, Tex., and the Coast Artillery School at Fort Scott, Calif."[158]

Although the 1950s saw Fort Sill lose the aviation school, the base expanded its artillery role to include "missile and atomic warhead training" to meet Cold War needs.[159] During the 1950s, the United States built several atomic cannons, field artillery guns capable of firing a nuclear warhead. Each was called "Atomic Annie." The only time an atomic artillery shell was fired was the May 25, 1953 test at Frenchman's Flat, Nevada, in which Fort

A 15-kiloton test fired from a 280-millimeter atomic cannon on May 25, 1953, at Frenchman's Flat, Nevada. This "Atomic Annie" is on display at Fort Sill. *Courtesy of National Nuclear Security Administration Nevada Site Office Photo Library.*

Sill personnel "fired a live 280-millimeter atomic round" from one of the atomic cannons. "The shell detonated 500 feet in the air with a 15 kiloton nuclear explosion, the same as the bomb that destroyed Hiroshima." The Atomic Annie used for this historic nuclear test is on display at Fort Sill.[160]

Another Cold War development found Fort Sill personnel develop the Honest John rocket as well as the Redstone and Corporal missiles, capable of carrying a nuclear payload. Additionally, the base saw the arrival of the "Polar Bears" of the Fourth Battalion, Thirty-First Infantry. The battalion was activated there for training "in joint combat tactics." The Polar Bears later moved to Fort Drum, New York. As the country transitioned into the Vietnam era, the artillery school began testing aerial rocket artillery for helicopters. Then, in 1966 and 1967, the artillery school helped develop "the Field Artillery Digital Automated Computer, commonly called FADAC, to compute fire direction data."[161] This put Fort Sill on the cutting edge for Army computer advancement.

Altus Air Force Base

Altus Army Air Field was another military installation necessary to fight World War II, and it began training pilots in 1943. Trainees learned to operate the Boeing-Stearman Kaydet T-17 as well as the North American T-9, then transferred elsewhere to train on the planes they would fly in the European and Pacific theaters. After the European war ended, the base was inactivated temporarily in May 1945. After the Korean War began, the need for fliers necessitated that Altus Air Force Base be reactivated, and it was on August 1, 1953. The C-47 Skytrain and the C-45 Expediter were the primary transport planes used for training.[162]

Throughout the 1950s, Altus Air Force Base "crews trained on the KC-97 Strato-freighter, a dual-purpose cargo and air refueling aircraft, and the first all-jet engine bomber, the B-47 Stratojet." Late that decade, they gave way to the B-52 Stratofortress and the KC-135 Stratotanker. Then, from 1962 to 1965, Altus Air Force Base was the hub for the twelve Atlas F intercontinental ballistic missile sites operated by the 577th Strategic Missile Squadron. In 1967, the C-141 Starlifter and the C-5 Galaxy were assigned to Altus Air Force Base. From the early 1970s and into the 1980s and 1990s, the KC-135, C-141 and C-5 were frequently seen in the skies near Altus in Jackson County.[163]

Through wars and rumors of wars, Oklahoma's military installations have readied personnel to fight for this country and defend freedom. In the process, Oklahoma communities near these installations have seen populations increase and jobs created. A few communities, unfortunately, have also felt the sting of base closure and the resulting exodus of affiliated personnel. All of these installations—Tinker Air Force Base, Vance Air Force Base, Clinton-Sherman Air Force Base, the U.S. Army Ammunition Plant, Fort Sill and Altus Air Force Base—served the nation well during the Cold War by preparing troops and air personnel to defend the nation and the free world during the greatest danger the world has ever faced.

THE POLITICIAN AND THE PILOT

CARL ALBERT AND THOMAS P. STAFFORD

As the Oklahoman who reached higher in government than any other, Carl Albert was twice just a heartbeat away from the presidency. Thomas P. Stafford became a star by being among the first humans to hover above the moon. Both men reached unprecedented heights in their chosen professions—Albert figuratively, Stafford literally. One a politician, the other a pilot, both were key Cold War figures.

CARL ALBERT

Born near McAlester in southeastern Oklahoma in 1908, less than a year after the state joined the Union, Albert's family moved to Bugtussle, and he later graduated from McAlester High School in 1927 as its valedictorian and student body president. That fall, he entered the University of Oklahoma in Norman, where he was a member of the Reserve Officers' Training Corps and the debate team, president of the student council, named outstanding male student and received a Phi Beta Kappa key before graduating in 1931 with a degree in government. Having been named a Rhodes Scholar, Albert took his OU degree to England, where he earned a law degree from Oxford and was a classmate of future secretary of state Dean Rusk. He returned to the United States, and during World War II, Albert served with the judge advocate general's (JAG) office within the army air corps, first in

Washington, D.C., then with General Douglas MacArthur's JAG office in the Pacific. Before transferring to the Pacific, Albert married Mary Harmon in August 1942.[164]

The couple relocated to McAlester following the war, and he ran for Congress in 1946, as the Cold War was heating up. That year, Oklahoma's Third Congressional District Democratic primary featured eight candidates. Albert's campaign slogan was "From a Cabin in the Cotton to Congress," and he won by only 330 votes. He went on to defeat his Republican opponent in the general election. He was sworn into the Eightieth Congress with two other now-famous freshmen: John Kennedy and Richard Nixon.[165]

Shortly after his arrival, a longtime House member, failing to recognize his new colleague and instead mistaking Albert for a page, "ordered him to take a batch of papers to his office."[166] Albert complied. His hard work and tenacity caused Speaker of the House Sam Rayburn to take notice, though. Rayburn named Albert to the leadership position of House Democratic whip in 1955, saying of his southeastern Oklahoma protégé, "I can tell big timber from small brush." Rayburn died in 1961, and after John McCormack became Speaker of the House, Albert was named Democratic House majority leader. While in this role, the nation underwent the shock of President Kennedy's assassination in 1963 and the war in Vietnam, the turmoil of which dissuaded incumbent president Lyndon Johnson from seeking reelection in 1968. Albert presided over the Democratic Party's chaotic national convention that year in Chicago as antiwar protestors clashed with police outside, and similar chaos dominated the proceedings inside.[167]

Then, in 1971, "when McCormack retired after [a] tumultuous tenure that had weathered clashes over education, civil rights, welfare programs, and Vietnam,"[168] Albert became Speaker of the House, a title he would hold for five years. The part of southeast Oklahoma where Albert was from is known as Little Dixie. Because Albert was only five foot four, he came to be known in Congress as "the Little Giant from Little Dixie," in part because he rose to the Speakership.[169]

The order of presidential succession matters a great deal, especially for the Speaker of the House when a vacancy arises in the office of the vice president. Such a vacancy occurred twice when Albert was Speaker during the Watergate controversy—first in 1973, when President Nixon's vice president Spiro Agnew resigned, then, less than a year later, when Nixon resigned and the presidency passed to Gerald Ford. In both instances, Carl Bert Albert from McAlester, Oklahoma, was a heartbeat away from

Democratic Congressional leaders are pictured after a breakfast meeting on Vietnam with President Lyndon Johnson on July 27, 1965. (*Left to right*) Representative Carl Albert, Vice President Hubert Humphrey, Speaker John McCormack (*speaking*), Representative Hale Boggs, Senator George Smathers and Senator Mike Mansfield. *Courtesy of the LBJ Presidential Library.*

the presidency and becoming the leader of the free world in the midst of the Cold War.[170]

During his thirty-year career in the House, Albert was forced to take stands on controversial issues. For example, Albert stood with President Johnson after the Tonkin Gulf Resolution "calling for the use of armed force in Southeast Asia. Mr. Albert spoke in favor of the resolution and said it was time for Americans to stand behind the president." Albert later walked back his endorsement of the war-authorizing resolution, saying that he had "no great enthusiasm for the Vietnam War." In fact, in "1973, Mr. Albert helped lead House efforts to block further military operations in Cambodia, Laos, North Vietnam and South Vietnam."[171]

Albert also had a front-row view of the most serious events of the Cold War, requiring the most consequential decisions from the U.S. government. In his autobiography, Albert wrote of Cold War crises during his time as House majority leader that found bipartisan support for President Kennedy's foreign policy in general and his handling of these crises in particular.

This included beating back Soviet leader Nikita Khrushchev's missile-backed threats to end Allied access to West Berlin by speeding "a resolution authorizing the president 'to prevent by whatever means may be necessary, including the force of arms,' any Soviet attempt to interfere with Western rights in Berlin."[172]

Albert was called to the White House on October 22, 1962, for a 5:00 p.m. meeting with President Kennedy, who was scheduled to address the nation in two hours. Kennedy told the House and Senate leaders who had assembled of the evidence that he had been shown that the Soviet Union was building missile sites in Cuba capable of firing nuclear weapons within easy reach of the United States. "He would inform the nation by television of the situation and announce his decision to 'quarantine' Cuba with a naval blockade to turn back the Soviet freighters" that were headed to the island nation with more Soviet weaponry as he worked to dismantle the missile sites and end the threat in Cuba. "As we sat there conferring, America's B-52 bombers, their bellies engorged with atomic bombs, already were in the air. The instant one landed for fuel and a fresh crew, another climbed into the sky." Before President Kennedy left the group of Congressional leaders to prepare for his television address, Albert told him that any concerns just voiced by his colleagues about Kennedy's course of action "would be forgotten. He was our president. He would get our support."[173]

Since his retirement from Congress in 1976, his home state has honored Albert in several ways. His alma mater, the University of Oklahoma, created the Carl Albert Congressional Research and Studies Center as a

> *nonpartisan institution that strengthens representative democracy through scholarship, learning, and service. Established in 1979 by the Oklahoma State Regents for Higher Education and the Board of Regents of the University of Oklahoma, the center is a living tribute to the ideals, leadership, and accomplishments of the honorable Carl Albert, native Oklahoman, University of Oklahoma alumnus, Rhodes Scholar, 46th Speaker of the U.S. House of Representatives.*[174]

Carl Albert State College in Poteau and Carl Albert High School in Oklahoma City also bear his name. There "is also a Carl Albert statue at the Federal Building and a monument to mark his birthplace."[175]

THOMAS P. STAFFORD

Born in Weatherford, Oklahoma, on September 17, 1930, Thomas P. Stafford graduated from Weatherford High School in 1948. He was accepted into the U.S. Naval Academy in Annapolis, Maryland, where he earned a bachelor of science degree with honors in 1952. Upon graduation, Stafford "was commissioned a second lieutenant in the United States Air Force."[176] Stafford married Linda Ann Dishman from Chelsea, Oklahoma.

Stafford was stationed at Connally Air Force Base in Waco, Texas, in 1953 and was later sent to Ellsworth Air Force Base in Rapid City, South Dakota, as part of the Fifty-Fourth Fighter Interceptor Squadron. In late 1955, he was transferred to Hahn Air Base in Germany, "where he performed the duties of pilot, flight leader, and flight test maintenance officer, flying F-86Ds." Stafford also received the Outstanding Graduate Award after his time as a student in the air force's Experimental Test Pilot School. He became an instructor and oversaw the writing of manuals for students and staff, and he coauthored the *Pilot's Handbook for Performance Flight Testing* and the *Aerodynamics Handbook for Performance Flight Testing.*[177]

NASA chose Stafford as one of the astronauts for the Gemini and Apollo projects in 1962, during the thick of the Cold War. The space race intensified in the late 1950s as the Soviet Union launched the first intercontinental ballistic missile and Sputnik. President Kennedy was determined to prevent the Soviet Union from dominating the skies, and space exploration became a national priority. In a June 1962 press conference, President Kennedy said he wished to fully fund the American space program: "I do not think the United States can afford to become second in space because I think that space has too many implications militarily, politically, psychologically, and all the rest." He alluded to the belief by many that the Soviet Union had a scientific and technological advantage over the United States. "I think the fact that the Soviet Union was…first in space in the fifties had a tremendous impact upon a good many people who were attempting to make a determination as to whether they could meet their economic problems without engaging in a Marxist form of government. I think the United States cannot permit the Soviet Union to become dominant in the sea of space."[178]

In late 1965, Stafford piloted Gemini 6 with fellow astronaut Wally Schirra during the first space rendezvous and closed to within a foot of Gemini 7, crewed by astronauts Frank Borman and Jim Lovell. In June 1966, he was commander of Gemini 9, piloted by Gene Cernan. On this mission, the crew was forced to rendezvous "with an alternate docking target after the Atlas [rocket] boosting their original Agena target failed." He oversaw the Apollo project between August 1966 and October 1968. In 1969, Stafford helped humanity get closer to a moon landing. In May that year, he "commanded the Apollo 10 lunar orbit flight…with John Young and Gene Cernan" and came within ten miles of the moon's surface, allowing the Apollo 11 team to become the first to land on the moon in July.[179] Additionally, Stafford was listed in the *Guinness Book of World Records* for reaching the highest speed ever achieved by humans when his Apollo 10 reentry craft reached "24,791 statute miles per hour."[180]

Stafford's fourth flight commanding an Apollo mission in July 1975—the Apollo-Soyuz Test Project—was the most significant for international relations. "He, Deke Slayton, and Vance Brand linked in orbit with a Soyuz carrying [Soviet] cosmonauts Alexei Leonov and Valery Kubasov,"[181] the first time that representatives of each country's space program met in space. According to NASA, this mission "ended the International space race."[182]

On November 4, 1975, Stafford took command of the Air Force Flight Test Center. Three years later, he became deputy chief of staff of research, development and acquisition at Air Force Headquarters in Washington, D.C. "In early 1979, he wrote the initial desired specifications on and started the advanced technology bomber ATB development," the program that led to the B-2, known to the public as the stealth bomber. Stafford also "initiated the AGM-129 Stealth Cruise Missile." Stafford retired from the U.S. Air Force in November 1979, having been promoted to the rank of major general.[183]

General Stafford received numerous awards from NASA, the Congressional Space Medal of Honor and the Veterans of Foreign Wars National Space Award, and he was inducted into the Astronaut Hall of Fame, the Oklahoma Commerce and Industry Hall of Honor, the National Aviation Hall of Fame and the Aerospace Walk of Honor. Named a distinguished U.S. Naval Academy graduate, he was also honored with the U.S. Air Force Lifetime Achievement Award. General Stafford has also been awarded several honorary degrees, including a doctorate of laws from Oklahoma State University, a doctorate of humane letters from the University of Oklahoma, a doctorate of science from Oklahoma City University, a doctorate of humanities from Oklahoma Christian College and a masters of humane letters from SWOSU in his hometown of Weatherford.[184]

In addition to granting General Stafford an honorary degree, SWOSU in Weatherford named a campus building in his honor. "The General Thomas P. Stafford Center is a 65,000-square-foot building dedicated in 1996…

Thomas P. Stafford's 1966 NASA photograph. *Courtesy of NASA.*

[and] contains the Bernhardt Lecture Hall, 10 classrooms, five computer labs and two seminar rooms. In addition, the building houses Student Financial Services, Admissions and Recruitment, Career Services, the Dean of Students, Information Technology Services, and the Everett Dobson School of Business and Technology."[185] Additionally, Stafford's hometown

The General Thomas P. Stafford Center on the campus of Southwestern Oklahoma State University in Weatherford. *Courtesy of the author.*

of Weatherford has embraced the general's legacy by opening the Stafford Air & Space Museum, featuring displays replete with artifacts donated by Stafford that chronicle his life and career as a pilot and an astronaut.[186]

Carl Albert and Thomas P. Stafford each strove for excellence in his chosen field at a critical time for the country and the world. Albert helped guide the government in its military and foreign policy decisions and during domestic and international crises when peace could easily have become war with the Soviet Union—a frightening prospect in a nuclear age. Stafford reached for the moon and stars and hit his mark at a time when we raced against the Soviets to be the first to conquer the final frontier of space. These notable Cold War Oklahomans represented the best that the state and country had to offer as they served with honor.

10

MAURICE HALPERIN

FROM SOONER SUBVERSIVE TO SOVIET SPY

Maurice Halperin stands in stark contrast to Carl Albert and Thomas P. Stafford. Albert and Stafford served this country with distinction, whereas Halperin betrayed it. Halperin was a University of Oklahoma professor in the late 1930s and early 1940s, when the state's governor and legislature began actively pursuing Communists in higher education. After Halperin fell under suspicion, he left the university for a job with the federal government's wartime intelligence agency. Still under a cloud of suspicion, Halperin eventually fled the country, never to return. Shortly after the Cold War ended, evidence emerged verifying the allegations made by his accusers that, during the 1930s, Maurice Halperin was a covert Oklahoma Communist, and during the 1940s, he betrayed his country by committing espionage for the Soviet Union.

Maurice Halperin graduated from Harvard in 1926 at twenty having studied languages, and he took a job teaching French and Spanish for the high school and junior college in Ranger, Texas, near Fort Worth. After a year in Ranger, Halperin was accepted at the University of Oklahoma, where he began graduate school in September 1927. Roy Temple House was chairman of the university's Modern Languages Department, and he began *Books Abroad*, a journal dedicated to writing English-language reviews of books that had been written in other languages. Halperin published reviews in *Books Abroad*, and through the journal, he was introduced to Marxism, which he admitted influenced him profoundly:

Part of the stuff that came in had very distinct Marxist orientations. This was the first time I got literature that had an explicitly Marxist analysis. It was fascinating, a new analytical approach, a new understanding of history....Intellectually it broadened my vision, especially of the contemporary world. Among them, books dealing with the Russian Revolution, which I never would have found on the stands in Norman. An accident, but I think it played a real role in my future development.[187]

With a master's degree from the University of Oklahoma in hand, in 1929, Halperin left Norman for the University of Paris to pursue a doctorate. While Halperin was finishing his work in France in 1931, House offered him a faculty position at the University of Oklahoma. Halperin happily accepted the offer to return to Norman.[188]

During the next ten years there, Halperin studied Latin America, and "at the same time, he began to drift leftward politically." In 1932, Halperin attended a speech delivered in Oklahoma City by Communist Party presidential candidate James Ford. Ford was black, and the crowd included both whites and blacks. "This was Oklahoma in 1932, and that sort of thing was simply not done there."[189] Halperin was impressed with the message of equality that he heard:

I don't recall anything spectacular about it. It wasn't concerned with the overthrow of the government but with the rights of the poor....I knew that this was a utopian little group here. Another thing that impressed me was the religious attachments that these people had to the cause that they were supporting. Religious almost in the literal sense because when they approved of something, they would shout "Amen!"[190]

As a young graduate student at the University of Oklahoma in the late 1920s, Halperin was introduced to the Marxist worldview. When he returned to Norman as a faculty member in the 1930s, he was introduced to Marx:

So I started reading Marx.....Marx made a tremendous impression and the impression had to do with maybe two or three things. One, his historical method seemed to throw a great searchlight on history. And number two, his critique of capitalism which I got not from Das Kapital, *which was just too much for me, but from essays and interpretations by other people. And of course his ethical concerns were expressed in such a convincing way. It was clear that I was dealing with a huge intellect. He was a giant.[191]*

Halperin wrote an article about exploitation of Mexican workers in *Current History*, and the article was quoted in a 1934 issue of *Time* magazine. As a result, he was invited to accompany a group of leftists traveling from New York to Cuba in the summer of 1935 to explore allegations "of atrocities by Cuba's strongman, Batista, in connection with a long-term strike there." When he arrived in his room aboard the ship sailing for Cuba, Halperin saw an issue of the Communist Party newspaper the *Daily Worker*. He said that he then realized that the fellows traveling with him were more than just fellow travelers. "So I could see some element of the Communist Party was involved in this thing."[192]

1926–27 Ranger College yearbook photograph of faculty member Maurice Halperin. *Courtesy of the author.*

Because the trip to Cuba, including a brief detention of the ship's passengers by Cuban police, was chronicled by passenger and leftist playwright Clifford Odets in the Marxist magazine *New Masses* shortly after the group returned to New York, word of the detention quickly arrived in Oklahoma. Just as quickly, University of Oklahoma president William Bizzell summoned Halperin to his office to explain his role in the affair. Bizzell reminded Halperin of the need for a good public image and ended the meeting without taking any action.[193]

The trip to Cuba among Communists put Halperin in the company of people with whom he increasingly shared a worldview. In the 1930s, he wanted the Democratic Party to oppose fascism in Europe, which caused him to support the foreign policy of the Communist Party USA. A supporter of FDR's New Deal domestically, by 1936 he was, by his own admission, a fellow traveler. For two years beginning in the fall of 1937, Halperin regularly contributed to a faculty column, the "Faculty Forum," in the University of Oklahoma's student newspaper, the *Oklahoma Daily*. He wrote mostly about the Roosevelt administration and world events, especially overseas fascism. Because the Soviet Union opposed fascism, Halperin gave Soviet leader Joseph Stalin a pass when the purge trials in the Soviet Union found innocents admitting guilt in supposed plots to undermine the Soviet government. Stalin, he wrote, was preferable to his fascist counterparts. However, when the Nazi-Soviet Pact was announced in 1939, Halperin went strangely silent and devoted no column inches to the alliance. He also chose not to comment on the September 1939 Soviet invasion of Poland and the subsequent invasion of Finland. Then, in 1940, he stopped writing his column altogether.[194]

During these years, Halperin was taking unpopular positions in Oklahoma, including supporting President Roosevelt's infamous court-packing plan that was ultimately rejected. Though the "press, the oil interests" and "most of the state Democratic Party were ranged against the president," Halperin went on record and signed a petition of support for the ill-fated presidential effort. Then he began lecturing around Norman defending "the Mexican government's action in expropriating American oil properties," followed by statewide lectures defending John Steinbeck's portrayal in *The Grapes of Wrath* of the shabby treatment migrants received as they moved west after being forced off their land. All of these stances were much further left than those of most Oklahomans.[195]

In 1938, Halperin made a financial decision that haunted him for years afterward. He spent hundreds of dollars and bought Soviet bonds from the Chase Manhattan Bank to earn the 7 percent interest that was advertised, more than twice the yield of American bonds at the time. Then, after the Nazi-Soviet Pact in 1939, Halperin decided to sell the bonds. Chase Manhattan sent the money to Halperin's bank along with paper notification to pay him that amount. Suspicious, the bank notified the FBI and University of Oklahoma president William Bizzell. According to Halperin, he was accused of being a Soviet spy, though nothing came of the incident then.[196]

Robert Wood, chairman of the Oklahoma Communist Party, was tried in the fall of 1940 for violating Oklahoma's criminal syndicalism act. This was a microcosm of nationwide anti-Communist sentiment that was seen in the actions of the House Un-American Activities Committee (HUAC), a Congressional committee chaired by Martin Dies of Texas. States like Oklahoma created their own versions of HUAC, dubbed "Little Dies Committees," to investigate local un-American activities, which, along with the conviction of Wood, alarmed state liberals and radicals. This fear that civil liberties were under attack was the impetus for the formation of the Oklahoma Federation for Constitutional Rights in October 1940. One of the executive committee members was Maurice Halperin.[197]

In January 1939, Oklahoma governor Leon Phillips claimed that professors at the University of Oklahoma in Norman were teaching Communist ideology, and he called for the firing of those professors.

Phillips's accusations led many associated with the University of Oklahoma to call for an investigation. Professors there believed Phillips's claim of subversives in their midst was based on participation by some faculty members in both the state's Federation for Constitutional Rights and a state civil rights symposium.[198]

While Governor Phillips sounded the alarm about state subversives, the Oklahoma legislature also acted. In January 1939, Tom Knight, state house member from Claremore, "authored a bill making it a crime to participate in any sit-down strike or teach un-American theories of government." Then, in a February joint meeting of the state legislature with Governor Phillips and Lieutenant Governor James Berry in the audience, the American Legion's national commander "called for a 'purge' of professors who teach subversive doctrine such as Communism or fascism, so America can achieve internal peace."[199]

Two events in 1940 triggered energetic anti-Communist reactions from the governor and, once the legislature was back in session in 1941, from that body as well. A constitutional rights conference was held on November 15, 1940, in Oklahoma City. Three days before the event was scheduled, Phillips held a press conference and warned University of Oklahoma faculty members not to attend. "The six professors scheduled to attend the conference included Dr. Charles M. Perry, Dr. John F. Bender, Dean Nicholas Comfort, Dr. Maurice Halperin, Dr. J. Rud Nielson, and Dr. Willard Z. Park." Most of those men were subpoenaed when the legislature met in January 1941 to investigate "subversive groups throughout the state."[200]

During the legislature's first week in session, House Bill 17, prohibiting Communist Party members from appearing on state ballots, was passed by the full house 118–0. However, the Oklahoma Federation for Constitutional Rights insisted the bill receive a public hearing. Unhappy with the state legislature's aggressive attempt to curb the rights of perceived subversives in early 1941, leaders of the Oklahoma Federation of Constitutional Rights forced a showdown. "On January 23…two University of Oklahoma (OU) professors, W.C. Randels (mathematics) and Maurice Halperin (Romance languages), appeared uninvited at a meeting of the Senate Committee on Privileges and Elections to press for hearings on the anticommunist bills." Halperin maintained that the federation did not intend to uphold Communism but instead to protect the political rights of all Oklahomans. At the end of January, state senator Joe Thompson introduced legislation to begin investigating the Communist Party in Oklahoma.[201]

The Senate Committee on Privileges and Elections, tasked with the Communist investigation, met for the first time on February 4, 1941, and seven University of Oklahoma faculty members were among the thirty-five individuals subpoenaed to testify. Governor Phillips was the first to take the stand, and he announced during his testimony that he had provided the FBI several documents concerning Oklahoma Communism in the previous two years.[202] Oklahoma's Little Dies Committee heard witness testimony throughout February. Testifying before the committee on the final day were University of Oklahoma philosophy professors Charles Perry and Gustav Mueller, education professor John Bender and modern languages professor Maurice Halperin.[203]

During his testimony, Halperin was asked if he knew any Communists, and he answered that he did not. He was asked if he was a Communist or had attended any Communist Party meetings, and he again answered negatively. He also denied that he "believe[d] in the Russian cause." Then the committee asked about the 1935 trip to Cuba, and as Halperin's biographer Don S. Kirschner relates, "his replies were more than a bit disingenuous." When asked the purpose of the trip, he said "to study the culture, the civilization and the political situation in Cuba." In response to a question about being arrested, "he replied that they had been 'detained,' and explained that the authorities 'preferred we did not land because the situation there was rather tense. They feared for our safety.' " This was untrue. Additionally, though Halperin was asked who accompanied him on the trip, he failed to mention the Communist presence among his fellow travelers.[204]

After the investigation was concluded, the Little Dies Committee reported its findings to the whole senate on May 7, 1941, and asserted that the Communist Party was "active in the state and engaged in the field of propaganda and agitation," that more than thirty local Communist Party chapters existed, that total party membership exceeded one thousand and that "Communists worked in all sections of the state." One of the committee's eleven recommendations was that the University of Oklahoma fire professor Maurice Halperin.[205] The issue was resolved, however, when Halperin accepted a job as a "Latin American analyst with the Office of Strategic Services [OSS], the predecessor to the CIA."[206]

In 1946, amid souring relations with the Soviet Union, Congress was receiving information about Communists in the OSS. One OSS official singled out was Maurice Halperin. Aware of the allegation, Halperin decided to leave the OSS and take a job representing the American Jewish Conference to the United Nations. One morning that same year, Halperin read in Drew Pearson's newspaper column that he faced indictment for espionage while with the OSS. Though startling, nothing came of this public allegation.[207]

Why wasn't more done by the U.S. government in light of the espionage allegation? In a word, laxity. Halperin wasn't the first American government official accused of spying without repercussions. In 1939, Laurence Duggan of the State Department was told by Undersecretary Sumner Welles that State had information that Duggan had passed classified department documents to a Soviet agent. Instead of firing and prosecuting Duggan, Welles told him to seek employment elsewhere. Not only did Duggan not leave the State Department, he was later named Secretary of State Cordell Hull's personal advisor, which allowed Duggan to continue spying for the Soviet Union during World War II.[208]

The American security laxity was influenced by both naïveté and the pressing issues of war. Communists in the 1930s and 1940s were seen by some "as just a bunch of youthful radicals posing no danger to anyone at home or abroad." And the OSS was just as blind to the dangers of Communist espionage as the State Department was during the war years. The director of the OSS was William "Wild Bill" Donovan. Though he later became intensely anti-Communist, during World War II, he was unconcerned where intelligence came from if it helped beat the Germans. Donovan once said that "I'd put Stalin on the OSS payroll if I thought it would help us defeat Hitler." He also "claimed that leftists were often the bravest spies and saboteurs." As Donovan put it, "Every man or woman who can hurt the Hun is okay with me."[209]

Even FBI director J. Edgar Hoover seemed unconcerned about the possibility of Communists with malign intentions penetrating the American government. Though aware of J. Peters, Hoover paid scant attention to the man who operated the Ware Group, an underground Communist group of New Dealers that included Alger Hiss, Nathaniel Weyl, Laurence Duggan and more than thirty-five others in Washington, D.C. By the late 1940s, Hoover regretted his inaction early in the decade. "Partly to compensate for his prior negligence, Hoover ignited a witch hunt long past when the witches were dead. In the early to mid-thirties, however, they were very much alive."[210]

So the OSS wasn't the only government agency that turned a blind eye to Soviet agents in its midst. Because of the blindness toward Soviet intentions during the 1930s and 1940s within the State Department, FBI and OSS, Halperin was allowed to walk away from the nation's wartime intelligence agency after having been accused of espionage and nobody batted an eye. The national feeling toward Communists in government would soon change, though, and 1950s America would prove to be much less hospitable toward Soviet sympathizers.

Halperin left the American Jewish Conference to take a job with Boston University in the Latin American Regional Studies Department. While in Boston, Halperin's life changed dramatically in 1953. In the era of McCarthyism, "the Senate Internal Security Subcommittee (SISS) began its investigations under Democratic Senator McCarran in 1952, but it continued them under Republican Senator Jenner early in 1953." These hearings found several professors asserting their Fifth Amendment right against self-incrimination during testimony, for which they were fired from their universities. Halperin was subpoenaed, and in March 1953, he testified before SISS. Asked if he had been a member of the Communist Party and if he had engaged in the kind of espionage activity that former Soviet spy-turned-informant Elizabeth Bentley had accused him of to the FBI and HUAC, as well as being asked about his political activities at the University of Oklahoma, his Cuba trip, the Soviet bond purchase and other matters, Halperin generally invoked the Fifth Amendment, though he did assert that he did not commit espionage.[211]

Shortly after Halperin's testimony, Nathaniel Weyl, an admitted former Communist, also testified before SISS. A New York City Communist, Weyl took a job in Washington, D.C., in 1933 in the federal Agricultural Adjustment Administration. While there, "he joined a secret Communist party cell, most of whose members were later identified by Whittaker Chambers. He left the New Deal in 1934 to work full time for the Communist party by organizing farm workers in the Midwest." Weyl testified that he learned of Halperin through Homer Brooks, who had worked as an official for the Communist Party in the American Southwest. Brooks told Weyl of Halperin's having "been 'accredited' as the Texas-Oklahoma representative of the Communist party to the Mexican Communist party." Even Halperin's biographer concedes that Weyl was credible. The former Communist's testimony supported charges that Halperin had been a Communist while a professor at the University of Oklahoma, his protestations to the contrary before the Sooner State's Little Dies Committee notwithstanding.[212]

In the fall of 1953, a story broke that drove Halperin from both Boston and the United States when, for the second time, he was publicly linked to espionage. This time, the accusation came from high officials in the federal government. On November 17, President Eisenhower's attorney general,

Herbert Brownell, testified before SISS and read a November 1945 letter from FBI director J. Edgar Hoover to President Truman "identifying a spy ring that had been functioning in Washington during the war." The substance of the letter came from a deposition provided to the FBI by Elizabeth Bentley, and Halperin was one of the spies named. The director of the FBI, through the attorney general of the United States, using correspondence that included the president of the United States, claimed that Maurice Halperin was guilty of espionage on behalf of the Soviet Union.[213]

The next day, Wednesday, November 18, 1953, Boston University suspended Halperin pending a university committee meeting the following week to clarify the issues in which he was involved. One week after his suspension from Boston University, Halperin and his wife, Edith, purportedly fearing for his job and his ability to gain other American employment should he be fired in such an uncertain political environment, left Boston for Mexico. If Halperin had been liaison to the Mexican Communist Party as the Texas-Oklahoma representative of the Communist Party USA during the 1930s, as Nathaniel Weyl had testified, Halperin would have had contacts there.[214]

Maurice Halperin's life changed dramatically when Elizabeth Bentley accused him of being a spy for the Soviet Union. He denied her allegations, just as he had denied being a Communist in testimony before Oklahoma's Little Dies Committee in 1941 and before the FBI in 1942 and 1947, yet he fled the United States "and spent years of exile in Mexico, the Soviet Union, and Cuba, before settling in Canada." Either Bentley lied or Halperin lied.[215]

Elizabeth Bentley joined the Communist Party in the 1930s, and she began working in "its underground apparatus in New York"[216] by decade's end. She answered to Jacob Golos, with whom she became romantically involved. Golos worked for the NKVD, a predecessor of the Soviet Union's KGB. During World War II, she made contacts with employees of multiple government agencies in Washington, D.C. After Golos died in 1943, she became leery of her NKVD superiors, and she became paranoid that the FBI would soon arrest her for espionage, so in late 1945, she went to the FBI and confessed.

She testified behind closed doors for a grand jury in 1947 and before two congressional committees (including HUAC) in July 1948, when her revelations became public knowledge for the first time. Eventually she named more than one hundred people, but subsequent investigations focused primarily on the more than two dozen who were still employed by the federal government when she began to talk to the FBI in 1945. One of them was Maurice Halperin.[217]

Bentley claimed that Halperin had been a member of the Communist Party when he lived in Oklahoma in the 1930s. She said that when Halperin arrived in Washington, D.C., after taking the OSS job, he and former University of Oklahoma colleague Willard Park contacted Bruce Minton of the leftist *New Masses* magazine "and told him that 'they desired to be placed in contact with some Communist in the East.' " Minton took this to Golos, who put them in touch with Bentley. She said that she first met with Halperin late in 1942 at Willard Park's home in Maryland, "at which time she 'arranged to collect Communist Party dues' from him." Shortly thereafter, "Golos went to Washington 'and apparently made arrangements with them on that occasion to be supplied…with certain information to which they had access in their respective offices.' "[218]

Bentley said that Halperin "passed along 'mimeographed bulletins and reports prepared by OSS on a variety of topics and also supplied excerpts from State Department cables to which he evidently had access.' " FBI files also included a letter from within the bureau to Director J. Edgar Hoover discussing this information, saying "that in Bentley's early contacts with Halperin 'he had apparently unlimited access to what she describes as daily cabled intelligence summaries compiled by the State Department.' " Bentley visited Washington every two weeks, and this letter states that "HALPERIN would have a two-weeks accumulation of such summaries and sometimes would turn them over physically to her, while at other times he would perhaps clip out a pertinent paragraph or two and hand it over to her." Bentley also said that after OSS security was tightened, Halperin was forced to take greater care not to be discovered conveying this information to her, so he "adopted the practice of personally typing digests of such information as he thought of interest."[219]

Bentley told government officials that Halperin would occasionally come to New York, where she and Golos would spend the evening with him dining and enjoying a show. She conceded that Halperin may have believed that the classified OSS information he was giving to her was destined for the Communist Party USA instead of the Soviet Union, though the law did not recognize a distinction. The Espionage Act of 1917—under which Julius and Ethel Rosenberg were convicted in 1951 and subsequently executed in 1953—outlawed transmission of classified documents to unauthorized personnel. If Bentley's allegations were true, Halperin violated the Espionage Act. After their last contact in 1944, Bentley was told by a Soviet contact that OSS director William Donovan confronted Halperin about being a spy, after which Halperin no longer met with his Soviet intelligence contact, and she lost track of him.[220]

Halperin biographer Don S. Kirschner sums up Bentley's allegations against Halperin:

> She had firsthand knowledge that Halperin was a member of the Communist party; that he paid party dues to her; that he passed along printed material from the OSS and the State Department from late 1942 or early 1943 until late 1944, approximately two years; and that he occasionally met her and her superior in New York City. She had hearsay information that it was he who had initiated the contact with Communists in Washington; that the material he gave to her was prized by the NKVD; and that Donovan was aware of Halperin's activities by 1945, and had confronted him with them. She also knew that Halperin had been at Oklahoma University, that Willard Park had been there with him, and that Park was now employed in Washington.[221]

From 1940 until 1949, the FBI kept a file on Halperin, though little in it backs up Bentley's allegations. The file includes a May 1940 allegation from an anonymous Norman source noting that Halperin was "a suspect in 'espionage and Communistic activities.' " Hoover notified the FBI's Oklahoma City office when Halperin went to work for the federal government in Washington in 1941, pointing out that he had been accused by many in Norman of having Communist beliefs. In February 1942, the FBI's Washington office questioned Halperin under oath, and he swore that he had never been a Communist Party member. This echoed his testimony the previous year to the Oklahoma Little Dies Committee.[222]

In his 1953 testimony before SISS, Nathaniel Weyl said that the Communist Party organizer for Oklahoma and Texas, Homer Brooks, told Weyl that Halperin was a Communist. Halperin told his biographer that he had never heard of Homer Brooks. In 1993, however, Weyl provided further information to Kirschner that he had not provided in his 1953 testimony that included details involving his late wife, Sylvia. Weyl informed Kirschner by letter that, in the 1930s, Sylvia had

> accepted the job of organization secretary (the no. 2 spot) of the Texas-Oklahoma district of the CP. When we went down to Mexico, Homer told her to take over Halperin's job as rep to the Mexican Party. She met with Halperin at our hotel. I seem to recall meeting him then, but was not present at her talk with him. She told me that he had been uncooperative and resentful at having been replaced.[223]

In a follow-up telephone conversation, Weyl said that the meeting with Halperin was in 1936 or 1937. In his letter to Kirschner, Weyl wrote that even if Halperin was not a "card-carrying" Communist Party member in the 1930s, that distinction was irrelevant, because "the criterion for the Communist movement at that time was not whether one carried a membership card," because neither of the Weyls did, "but whether or not one accepted the discipline of the party and understood its ideology and line. If Dr. Halperin says he was never a party member, this may be a semantic issue without too much substance." After Kirschner confronted Halperin with this information during the writing of the biography, Halperin claimed that though he had met Nathaniel Weyl while in Mexico conducting journalistic research, he never met Sylvia, and he was not a representative to the Mexican Communist Party. However, Halperin had previously told Kirschner that he had, in fact, met Sylvia Weyl in Mexico. Whether Halperin was mistaken or lying, former Communist Nathaniel Weyl implicated Maurice Halperin in 1953 and again forty years later as a Communist during the 1930s while Halperin was a faculty member at the University of Oklahoma.[224]

Unfortunately for Kirschner, he did not have the benefit of information provided by Venona when he published his biography of Halperin. Venona was the name of a top-secret American program begun late in 1943 to decipher encrypted messages sent from Soviet diplomats in the United States to Moscow. Its hidden fifty-year existence was revealed to the American public in 1995. These deciphered messages showed that the Soviet Union, though a wartime ally, had, since 1942, placed at least "349 citizens, immigrants, and permanent residents of the United States" as spies in the American government and military, including the Manhattan Project. Spies such as assistant treasury secretary Harry Dexter White and presidential aide Lauchlin Currie were highly placed American government officials. Another was Maurice Halperin. Venona shows that Halperin, while employed with the OSS, "turned over hundreds of pages of secret American diplomatic cables to the KGB."[225]

Venona corroborates Elizabeth Bentley's description of Halperin's espionage productivity. Halperin specialized in providing Soviet intelligence "sensitive dispatches that were furnished to the OSS." In all, twenty-two decoded Venona messages detail Halperin's participation in espionage for the Soviet Union.

Halperin handed to the Soviets U.S. diplomatic cables regarding Turkey's policies toward Romania, State Department instructions to the U.S.

ambassador in Spain, U.S. embassy reports about Morocco, reports from Ambassador John Winant in London about the internal stance of the Polish government-in-exile toward negotiations with Stalin, reports on the U.S. government relationship with the many competing French groups and personalities in exile, reports of peace feelers from dissident Germans being passed on by the Vatican, U.S. perceptions of Tito's activities in Yugoslavia, and discussions between the Greek government and the United States regarding Soviet ambitions in the Balkans.[226]

In addition to compiling diplomatic information for Soviet sources, Halperin also slanted OSS reports to favor the Communist perspective.[227]

Halperin's inconsistent answers about Sylvia Weyl were not the only contradictory answers that he gave his biographer. Halperin told the FBI in 1947 that he was not a Communist, had never met Elizabeth Bentley and had never communicated with Soviet intelligence agents. Yet Halperin told Kirschner in the 1990s that he had met with Bentley but only in her capacity as assistant for Earl Browder, head of the Communist Party USA, and he never passed classified documents to her.[228]

Soviet intelligence gave code names to American assets and used those names in its communications. Halperin's code name was "Hare," and it was included in a November 23, 1945 message from Moscow listing thirteen agents with whom Anatoly Gorsky, a Soviet agent working in the United States, was to discontinue contact because of Elizabeth Bentley's confession of Soviet espionage to the FBI earlier that month.[229]

The U.S. government was unwilling to reveal the existence of Venona, so prosecutors pursued cases against spies in the 1940s and 1950s without the program's information. Without corroborating evidence, though, the government was often unable to bring those named to trial, much less get a guilty verdict. "Four of those Bentley named did testify, denied her charges, but then put themselves beyond prosecution for perjury by leaving the United States," including "Duncan Lee, Frank Coe, and Lauchlin Currie." The fourth was Maurice Halperin. Though Maurice Halperin denied Elizabeth Bentley's allegations about his involvement with Communism and Soviet espionage, Venona—which implicated Julius and Ethel Rosenberg, Harry Dexter White and Alger Hiss, among many others, in Soviet espionage— shows that Bentley told the truth and Halperin lied.[230]

Maurice Halperin swore under oath in the 1940s and 1950s that he was not a Communist, that he had never met Elizabeth Bentley and that he had never made contact with any Soviet intelligence agents or spied for the Soviet Union. Bentley and Nathaniel Weyl, on the other hand, testified that Halperin was a Communist in the 1930s while he was a University of Oklahoma professor, and Bentley testified that Halperin later engaged in espionage for the Soviet Union. Despite his denials in sworn testimony and to his biographer, Venona confirmed Halperin's Communist activity and Soviet espionage. Even if the search for Communists in Oklahoma and the nation was largely a baseless witch hunt—though Venona shows that that assessment may deserve *some* reevaluation—Halperin's case is an example of the aphorism that even a broken clock is right twice a day. Maurice Halperin was exposed as a Sooner subversive who became a Soviet spy.

11

PHOTO NOT AVAILABLE

Maurice Halperin didn't like having his picture taken.

Finding photographs of Halperin has proven challenging. So far, I've only seen four: his 1926–27 Ranger (Texas) College yearbook photo; a photo of him and his wife in 1976 that is part of Simon Fraser University's archives; a profile photo of him holding a violin at the Simon Fraser University website; and a photo on the cover of his biography.

Lance Hawvermale and Brandi Faulkner at Ranger College provided the yearbook photo. Thanks to them, I know what Halperin looked like in his early twenties. I don't know how old the violin-playing Halperin was in the Simon Fraser photograph, but he died one month before his eighty-ninth birthday in 1995, and I suspect that he was in his eighties on the biography cover. I searched for a photo of him from his days in Norman at the University of Oklahoma as both a student and faculty member and failed. Retired OU history professor David Levy literally wrote the book on the university, and he was familiar with Halperin's story. I contacted David, who graciously searched for a yearbook photo of Halperin during his twelve years as a graduate student and faculty member at OU, 1927–29 and 1931–41. He found nothing.

David also searched for a photo from Halperin's OU personnel file. Again, nothing.

Since Halperin left OU and took a job in 1942 with what became the Office of Strategic Services, I contacted the National Archives in Washington, D.C., the repository of OSS archives. The National Archives photo search proved equally unfruitful.

Halperin found employment with Boston University after his OSS service ended, so I contacted the university. The archival search for a photo of Halperin during his tenure turned up nothing. It's as though Halperin purposely avoided having his picture taken from the late 1920s until he left Boston, and the United States, for good in 1953. I even contacted the publisher of Halperin's biography and was told that it didn't have any photos. This must be why no photos appear in the biography, which is strange.

So why was Halperin loath to mug for a camera? There are, of course, many possibilities. I can't help wondering, though, if, given what we know about him, he avoided having his picture taken because of his role in the Communist Party and his desire to aid the Soviet Union.

The evidence shows that Halperin was a functionary for the Oklahoma-Texas Communist Party in the 1930s while on the University of Oklahoma faculty. Yet he repeatedly, and under oath, swore that he wasn't a Communist. While it's true that the political climate in Oklahoma at the time suggested that he avoid admitting being a party member, I suspect that more was involved.

Evidence indicates that he engaged in covert Communist Party activity in Oklahoma, Texas and Mexico in the 1930s. Evidence also indicates that he was a dues-paying Communist Party member when he went to work for the OSS in Washington, D.C., in the 1940s. Evidence also shows that he spied for the Soviet Union. What we don't know is when he began his Communist Party activity or how. Was he recruited when he was at Harvard as an undergraduate and tasked with working for the party in the American Southwest? That would explain why Halperin would leave Boston for Ranger, Texas—Halperin's stated desire to see and experience new things notwithstanding.

Of course, he allowed his picture to be taken for the 1926–27 Ranger College yearbook. Was this because he lacked party discipline? Or was this before he decided to work for the Communist Party? Whatever the reason, the lack of photographs from his twelve years in Norman suggests that by the late 1920s, he decided to avoid being photographed.

Even though the Great Depression had begun and jobs were hard to come by in 1931, that a Boston native left the East Coast for Ranger, Texas, then moved to Norman, Oklahoma, left to earn a doctorate in Paris, France, then returned to Norman, is eye-raising. Was it because he'd already established himself with the Communist Party in the region by 1931? Or because he wanted to?

The more innocent explanation that he was just happy to land a job when they were scarce may be correct, but the evidence provided by Nathaniel Weyl, Elizabeth Bentley and Venona, plus his apparent photographic shyness, suggests that he knew that his work for the Communist Party was in the American Southwest and returning to Oklahoma—and avoiding cameras—would facilitate that work.

That work was viewed as a prelude to the Cold War by some, the start of the Cold War by others.

As professors John Earl Haynes and Harvey Klehr point out, though a wartime ally, the Soviet Union behaved like this country's enemy in the years before and during World War II as it placed hundreds of spies inside the United States throughout the 1930s and 1940s, including many in the government.[231] In fact, author Katie Marton describes the 1930s as "the peak period of Soviet infiltration of the upper reaches of both the US and British governments."[232] The extent of Soviet agents' attempting to illegally access classified U.S. government documents and influence American foreign policy to advantage the Soviet Union then has led some to maintain that Stalin's American offensive started the Cold War years before World War II ended.[233]

Regardless of its start date, we now know that Maurice Halperin played a role in the Cold War by covertly advancing the cause of Communism while at the University of Oklahoma as Stalin's spies were being placed in sensitive government positions. Then Halperin took his Communism to a new level and advanced the cause of the Soviet Union by committing espionage as one of those well-placed spies in the U.S. government.

As this book shows, the Cold War had a profound impact on the lives of Oklahomans who lived through it. This included Oklahomans who built Atlas missile sites—and those Oklahomans who lived with them for three years, wondering if they'd ever be launched—Oklahomans who trained for civil defense to help themselves and others survive a nuclear attack, and military personnel and civilians who trained at and operated Oklahoma's military installations.

Maurice Halperin helped supply the demand for Oklahoma's—and the nation's—Cold War offense and defense by advancing the cause of Communism and the Soviet Union, first from Oklahoma, then from Washington, D.C.

12

COLD WAR LEGACY

T he Cold War ended with the dissolution of the Soviet Union in 1991. The ideological conflict between the United States and the Soviet Union lasted more than four decades and left its imprint on every region of the United States, including Oklahoma. With the advent of nuclear weapons, the Cold War became increasingly frightening as the world's two superpowers sought to defend themselves and advance their interests. "As the ideological battles played out, technological advances in weaponry increased the threat of thermonuclear holocaust."[234]

Just three years after World War II ended, the Strategic Air Command made Offutt Air Force Base, near Omaha, Nebraska, its headquarters. "SAC served as the air arm of the nation's offensive strategy for waging nuclear war, and it existed as an icon of American military power for the duration of the" decades-long Cold War. SAC expanded its presence in the middle of the country with "longrange bombers, such [as] the B-36 and B-52, planes that were capable of deployment into Soviet airspace." These bombers were supplanted in importance by intercontinental ballistic missiles such as the Atlas, which was deployed near air force bases in states that included Oklahoma, Texas and Kansas. As was the case in Oklahoma, these military installations and the Atlas missile sites attached to them "served as economic engines, providing well-paid and secure civilian support employment to local inhabitants in host communities."[235]

As discussed in chapter 2, though economically advantageous for the states and localities that built the Atlas sites and housed the missiles, and militarily advantageous for the nation in defending against and deterring possible attack, building the Atlas sites proved dangerous. More than fifty people died while building ICBM sites across several states, including three who died building the Atlas sites near Oklahoma's Altus Air Force Base. These were not the only American Cold War fatalities.

Americans also died fighting wars to stop Communist aggression in Korea and Vietnam. Of the more than 36,000 Americans who died fighting in Korea, 625 were from Oklahoma.[236] Of the more than 58,000 Americans who lost their lives serving the United States in the Vietnam War, 987 were from Oklahoma.[237] Though the United States was never officially at war with the Soviet Union during the Cold War, that conflict inspired American involvement in war abroad and defense at home that cost thousands of American lives. For the loved ones of those Americans who gave the last full measure of devotion—including those from Oklahoma—the loss is part of the Cold War's legacy.

Though in real terms the cost of human life is incalculable, the cost in lives lost was nevertheless high. The cost in dollars, which is calculable, was also high. "By 1995 the costs associated with the cold war had exceeded $5 trillion."[238]

A more pedestrian aspect of the Cold War's legacy in Oklahoma includes the discarded Atlas F intercontinental ballistic missile sites. All were sold after the Atlas program was phased out in 1965. Some are owned by private individuals. Others are owned by school districts that use them for agriculture education facilities. One site in southwest Oklahoma is a man's house. In fact, anyone willing to pay the asking price would likely be able to buy an Atlas site that formerly housed an ICBM. The man who lives in the Atlas F site in southwest Oklahoma bought it in 1999. As recently as 2017, an Atlas F site in New York was listed for sale. In 1997, it was purchased for $160,000. Then, in 2015, it was sold for $575,000. The 2017 asking price: $3 million. An Atlas site near Topeka, Kansas, was sold in the 1980s for $48,000, and the 2017 asking price was $3.2 million.[239]

As the nation employed civil defense measures in the hopes of surviving a nuclear attack, Oklahomans sprang into action. Public fallout shelters were identified and stocked, home shelters were built, and local civil defense units formed and planned for the unimaginable. Even high school students got involved, and college campuses found faculty teaching civil defense–related courses and preparing to survive nuclear attack. Part of Oklahoma's Cold War legacy is holes in buildings that once held fallout shelter signs; storage facilities with surplus fallout shelter supplies like empty water drums, medical equipment and radiation-detecting equipment; and home shelters used for storage and protection from severe weather. Civil defense preparedness, like offensive preparedness, also cost. Oklahoma "emerged from its cold war experience with deep ties to the federal defense budget, and with fallout shelters now used for storing canned goods and for refuge from tornadoes."[240]

The Cold War ended without a nuclear holocaust endangering civilization. As with any event that fades with the passing of time, the Cold War is a distant memory to some and nothing more than an era only known through history books by those too young to remember. It was, however, a dangerous time for Oklahoma, the nation and the world. Fortunately, through the leadership of Presidents Truman, Eisenhower, Kennedy and others, nuclear war was averted more than once as rational men chose peace over war and life over national death in several crises. Our task is to remember the events, the sacrifices, the stakes, the failures, the successes and the lessons learned so that we don't repeat them.

The Cold War began with uncertainty. Nobody knew how long it would last or if it would end peacefully or amid the ruins of a nuclear war. The American foreign policy that guided the nation through the Cold War was begun under President Truman and, in large measure, continued by all future presidents, both Democrat and Republican. Having lived through the entire Cold War, Clark Clifford, former counsel to President Truman, wrote these words about that policy in the early 1990s: "the policy that truly succeeded was born…when, in less than three years, President Truman unveiled the Truman Doctrine, the Marshall Plan, [and] NATO." Then, in the course of "the next forty years, the essential core of President Truman's policies survived…the four great challenges of…the Korean War, McCarthyism, Vietnam, and Watergate—and was accepted as the framework of our foreign policy by every President from Eisenhower to [George H.W.] Bush."[241]

Oklahoma and Oklahomans played key Cold War roles. As politicians, military personnel and civilians contributing to offensive preparedness, defensive preparedness and government domestic and foreign policy—plus at least one traitor who aided the nation's primary Cold War adversary—Oklahomans are part of the nation's Cold War legacy. Their efforts, and the record of their efforts, in addition to the military installations that continue to operate in the state and the one that doesn't, plus the Atlas missile silos and converted fallout shelters that dot Oklahoma's landscape, are all part of the Cold War's legacy in Oklahoma. Learning about these things reminds us who we are.

NOTES

Introduction

1. John F. Kennedy, "Address before the General Assembly of the United Nations, September 25, 1961," John F. Kennedy Presidential Library and Museum, accessed February 22, 2019, https://www.jfklibrary.org/archives/other-resources/john-f-kennedy-speeches/united-nations-19610925.

Chapter 1

2. Stephen E. Ambrose and Douglas G. Brinkley, *Rise to Globalism: American Foreign Policy Since 1938* (London: Penguin Books, 2011), 53.
3. Ibid., 54–56.
4. "Churchill's Iron Curtain Speech," Westminster College, accessed July 23, 2018, https://www.westminster-mo.edu/explore/history-traditions/IronCurtainSpeech.html.
5. Ambrose and Brinkley, *Rise to Globalism*, 76–82.
6. Ibid., 81, 83.
7. David McCullough, *Truman* (New York: Simon & Schuster, 1992), 582.
8. Ibid., 561–62.
9. Ibid., 562, 563.
10. Ibid., 565, 583.

11. Ibid., 566.

12. Ambrose and Brinkley, *Rise to Globalism*, 98–99.

13. Richard Reeves, *Daring Young Men: The Heroism and Triumph of the Berlin Airlift, June 1948–May 1949* (New York: Simon & Schuster, 2010), 274.

14. Ambrose and Brinkley, *Rise to Globalism*, 101.

15. McCullough, *Truman*, 747–49.

16. Ibid., 742–44, 749.

17. Ibid., 749, 757, 761–63.

18. Ibid., 772; Ambrose and Brinkley, *Rise to Globalism*, 772.

Chapter 2

19. John C. Lonnquest and David F. Winkler, *To Defend and Deter: The Legacy of the United States Cold War Missile Program* (Rock Island, IL: Defense Publishing Service, 1996), 65–66, http://www.atlasmissilesilo.com/Documents/Development/AZ-D-T-999-99-ZZ-00002_ToDefendAndDeter_TheLegacyOfTheUnitedStatesColdWarMissileProgram.pdf (accessed October 19, 2016).

20. Ibid., 67.

21. Ibid., 77.

22. Ibid., 210–11.

23. Ibid., 220.

24. Ibid., 215.

25. Ibid., 220–24.

26. Ibid., 220.

27. Ibid.

28. Ibid., 406.

29. *The City of Altus Salutes Altus Air Force Base* (Austin: Base Guides, 1964), http://www.atlasmissilesilo.com/Documents/Operational/AtlasF/577thSMS/AF-D-O-577-99-AL-00001_577thSMS_BaseHandoutBooklet.pdf (accessed October 19, 2016).

30. Lonnquest and Winkler, *To Defend and Deter*, 79.

31. Ibid., 80–81.

32. Ibid., 83.

33. S.C. Wood, "History of the Altus Area Office: 14 March 1960–28 April 1962" (Altus, OK: U.S. Army Corps of Engineers, Ballistic Missile Construction Office, 1962), 1:3, 9, http://www.atlasmissilesilo. com/Documents/ConstructionHistory/AtlasF/577thSMS/AF-D-

C-577-99-AL-00001_577thSMS_ConstructionHistory_Volume1.pdf (accessed October 25, 2016).

34. Ibid., 19.

35. S.C. Wood, "History of the Altus Area Office: 14 March 1960–28 April 1962" (Altus, OK: U.S. Army Corps of Engineers), Construction Summary, A-1, http://www.atlasmissilesilo.com/Documents/ConstructionHistory/AtlasF/577thSMS/AF-D-C-577-99-AL-00004_577thSMS_ConstructionHistorySummary.pdf (accessed October 25, 2016).

36. S.C. Wood, "History of the Altus Area Office: 14 March 1960–28 April 1962" (Altus, OK: U.S. Army Corps of Engineers, Ballistic Missile Construction Office, 1962), 2:19, http://www.atlasmissilesilo.com/Documents/ConstructionHistory/AtlasF/577thSMS/AF-D-C-577-99-AL-00002_577thSMS_ConstructionHistory_Volume2.pdf (accessed October 25, 2016).

37. Lonnquest and Winkler, *To Defend and Deter*, 406.

38. Wood, "History of the Altus Area Office," 2:58.

39. Wood, "History of the Altus Area Office," Construction Summary, A-2.

40. Lonnquest and Winkler, *To Defend and Deter*, 82.

41. Wood, "History of the Altus Area Office," 2:136–38.

42. Ibid., 148–50.

43. Ibid., 151.

44. Jerry Brewer, interview by the author, November 30, 2016.

45. Ibid.

46. S.C. Wood, "History of the Altus Area Office: 14 March 1960–28 April 1962" (Altus, OK: U.S. Army Corps of Engineers, Ballistic Missile Construction Office, 1962), 3:172, http://www.atlasmissilesilo.com/Documents/ConstructionHistory/AtlasF/577thSMS/AF-D-C-577-99-AL-00003_577thSMS_ConstructionHistory_Volume3.pdf (accessed October 25, 2016).

47. Thomas C. Reed, *At the Abyss: An Insider's History of the Cold War* (New York: Random House, 2004), 159.

48. "Only 10 Percent in Area 'Alive'," *Altus Times-Democrat*, May 4, 1960, https://news.google.com/newspapers?nid=LpWf3qrnWeoC&dat=19600504&printsec=frontpage&hl=en (accessed October 24, 2016).

49. "Nikita Asserts Pilot Confesses to Spy Mission," *Altus Times-Democrat*, May 8, 1960, https://news.google.com/newspapers?nid=LpWf3qrnWeoC&dat=19600508&printsec=frontpage&hl=en (accessed October 24, 2016).

50. "Work Begins on Lone Wolf Site," *Altus Times-Democrat*, May 9, 1960, https://news.google.com/newspapers?nid=LpWf3qrnWeoC&dat=1960 0509&printsec=frontpage&hl=en (accessed October 24, 2016).

51. "Two Sites Run into Water, Rock Slowup," *Altus Times-Democrat*, June 5, 1960, https://news.google.com/newspapers?nid=LpWf3qrnWeoC&d at=19600605&printsec=frontpage&hl=en (accessed October 24, 2016).

52. "Company Men Visit Base, Project Sites," *Altus Times-Democrat*, July 18, 1960, https://news.google.com/newspapers?nid=LpWf3qrnWeoC&dat =19600718&printsec=frontpage&hl=en (accessed October 24, 2016)

53. " 'Great Debate' on Schedule for Tonight," *Altus Times-Democrat*, September 26, 1960, https://news.google.com/newspapers?nid=Lp Wf3qrnWeoC&dat=19600926&printsec=frontpage&hl=en (accessed October 25, 2016).

54. "Kennedy Visit Leaves Demos More Hopeful," *Altus Times-Democrat*, November 4, 1960, https://news.google.com/newspapers?nid=LpWf3q rnWeoC&dat=19601104&printsec=frontpage&hl=en (accessed October 25, 2016).

55. "Missile Site Worker Killed," *Altus Times-Democrat*, November 4, 1960, https://news.google.com/newspapers?nid=LpWf3qrnWeoC&dat=1960 1104&printsec=frontpage&hl=en (accessed October 25, 2016).

56. "Silo Worker Dies in Fall," *Altus Times-Democrat*, December 28, 1960, https://news.google.com/newspapers?nid=LpWf3qrnWeoC&dat=1960 1228&printsec=frontpage&hl=en (accessed October 25, 2016).

57. *Altus Times-Democrat*, April 17, 1961, https://news.google.com/newspap ers?nid=LpWf3qrnWeoC&dat=19610417&printsec=frontpage&hl=en; *Altus Times-Democrat*, April 18, 1961, https://news.google.com/newspap ers?nid=LpWf3qrnWeoC&dat=19610418&printsec=frontpage&hl=en (accessed October 25, 2016)

58. "Launch Control Center at Snyder Turned to AF," *Altus Times-Democrat*, June 1, 1961, https://news.google.com/newspapers?nid=LpWf3qrnWe oC&dat=19610601&printsec=frontpage&hl=en (accessed October 25, 2016).

59. Ibid.

60. "Defense Chief Cites Terrible Nuclear Toll," *Altus Times-Democrat*, August 1, 1961, https://news.google.com/newspapers?nid=LpWf3qrnWeoC&d at=19610801&printsec=frontpage&hl=en (accessed October 25, 2016).

61. "Snyder Silo Is Signed to AF," *Altus Times-Democrat*, August 1, 1961.

62. Ibid.

63. Ibid.

64. "Potentially Hot Showdown Nearing; Russia Claims U.S. Sets Stage for War," *Altus Times-Democrat*, October 23, 1962, https://news.google.com/newspapers?nid=LpWf3qrnWeoC&dat=19621023&printsec=frontpage&hl=en (accessed October 25, 2016).

65. "SAC Missile Chronology: 1939–1988" (Offutt Air Force Base, NE: Office of the Historian, Headquarters Strategic Air Command, May 1, 1990), 36, 37, http://www.atlasmissilesilo.com/Documents/SAC/MI-D-T-999-99-ZZ-00001_SACMissileChronology_1939-1988.pdf (accessed October 25, 2016).

66. "Altus Base Silent on Its Activity," *Altus Times-Democrat*, October 23, 1962, https://news.google.com/newspapers?nid=LpWf3qrnWeoC&dat=19621023&printsec=frontpage&hl=en (accessed October 25, 2016).

67. "Civil Defense Plan Reviewed," *Altus Times-Democrat*, October 23, 1962.

68 "Cache Site Liquid Oxygen Line Leak Is 'Contained'," *Altus Times-Democrat*, October 29, 1962, https://news.google.com/newspapers?nid=LpWf3qrnWeoC&dat=19621029&printsec=frontpage&hl=en (accessed October 25, 2016).

69. "Frederick Site on Fire: None Hurt in Missile Explosion," *Altus Times-Democrat*, May 14, 1964, https://news.google.com/newspapers?nid=LpWf3qrnWeoC&dat=19640514&printsec=frontpage&hl=en (accessed October 25, 2016).

70. "SAC Missile Chronology: 1939–1988," 43–44, 47.

71. Lonnquest and Winkler, *To Defend and Deter*, 137–38.

72. Ibid., 541–42.

73. Zeke Campfield, "Hobart Man Fixing Up Old Missile Silo as a Home," *Oklahoman*, December 19, 2009, http://newsok.com/article/feed/115076 (accessed October 18, 2016).

74. Ibid.

75. "Historical Vignette 032—The Corps Built the Launch Sites for Atlas ICBM," U.S. Army Corps of Engineers, accessed October 14, 2016, http://www.usace.army.mil/About/History/Historical-Vignettes/Military-Construction-Combat/032-Atlas-ICBM/.

76. Address by President Kennedy, October 22, 1962, quoted in Robert F. Kennedy, *Thirteen Days: A Memoir of the Cuban Missile Crisis* (New York: W.W. Norton and Company, 1969), 168.

Chapter 3

77. Jerry Burns, "How Grandpa Got to Retirement and Why He Loves It There," accessed July 19, 2018, http://www.frontiernet.net/~bobhc/.
78. Ibid.
79. Jerry Burns, "Burns at Altus AFB, Oklahoma," accessed July 19, 2018, http://www.frontiernet.net/~bobhc/Altus_1.html.
80. Ibid.
81. Ibid.
82. Ibid.
83. "DEFCON DEFense CONdition," Federation of American Scientists, accessed July 20, 2018, https://fas.org/nuke/guide/usa/c3i/defcon.htm.
84. Jerry Burns, "Burns at Altus AFB, Oklahoma," accessed July 19, 2018, http://www.frontiernet.net/~bobhc/Altus_1.html.
85. Ibid.

Chapter 4

86. "577th SMS, Altus AFB: Accidents," *Atlas Missile Silo*, accessed July 20, 2018, http://www.atlasmissilesilo.com/accidents_577thsms_site6.htm; "Terms and Definitions," *Atlas Missile Silo*, accessed July 20, 2018, http://www.atlasmissilesilo.com/terms_definitions.htm.
87. "577th SMS, Altus AFB: Accidents"; "Terms and Definitions."
88. "577th SMS, Altus AFB: Accidents."

Chapter 5

89. Landry Brewer and Michael Dobbs, "The Missiles of Oklahoma," YouTube video, 1:46:19, from the Missiles of Oklahoma seminar, October 26, 2017, posted by the SWOSU Libraries, March 9, 2018, https://www.youtube.com/watch?v=zS2OVJUQcHw.
90. Galen Culver, "Oklahoma's Abandoned Missile Sites Are Getting Above Ground Recognition after More than 50 Years," KFOR, last updated June 29, 2017, https://kfor.com/2017/06/28/oklahomas-abandoned-missile-sites-are-getting-above-ground-recognition-after-more-than-50-years/.

Chapter 6

91. B. Wayne Blanchard, *American Civil Defense 1945–1984: The Evolution of Programs and Policies*, Monograph Series 1985, vol. 2, no. 2 (Emmitsburg, MD: National Emergency Training Center, 1986), 2–3, http://www.civildefensemuseum.com/docs/AmericanCivilDefense1945-1984.pdf (accessed April 10, 2018).

92. U.S. Department of Homeland Security National Preparedness Task Force, *Civil Defense and Homeland Security: A Short History of National Preparedness Efforts* (Washington, D.C.: Homeland Security, National Preparedness Task Force, 2006), 9–10, https://training.fema.gov/hiedu/docs/dhs%20 civil%20defense-hs%20-%20short%20history.pdf (accessed April 19, 2018); see also B. Wayne Blanchard, *American Civil Defense 1945–1984*, 4–6.

93. Blanchard, *American Civil Defense*, 6–7.

94. Evan Thomas, *Ike's Bluff: President Eisenhower's Secret Battle to Save the World* (New York: Little, Brown, 2012), 270, 272–74.

95. Ibid., 274.

96. Landry Brewer, "The Missiles of Oklahoma: Southwest Oklahoma's Role in the American Cold War Nuclear Arsenal, 1960–65," *Chronicles of Oklahoma* 95, no. 3 (Fall 2017): 268.

97. "Special Message to Congress on Urgent National Needs," quoted in Blanchard, *American Civil Defense 1945–1984*, 7–8.

98. Blanchard, *American Civil Defense 1945–1984*, 8.

99. "Defense Chief Cites Terrible Nuclear Toll," *Altus Times-Democrat*, August 1, 1961.

100. James Gregory, "In the Fallout Shelter: Civil Defense in Stillwater," *Stillwater Living Magazine* (October 11, 2017), 3–4, http://stillwaterliving.com/in-the-fallout-shelter-civil-defense-in-stillwater/ (accessed April 17, 2018).

101. Ibid., 4–5.

102. Ibid., 5–6; Joe Wertz, "From Nuclear Fallout to Tornadoes, A Shifting View of Public Shelter Policy in Oklahoma," StateImpact Oklahoma, June 27, 2013, accessed July 19, 2018, https://stateimpact.npr.org/oklahoma/2013/06/27/the-evolution-of-public-shelter-policy-in-oklahoma/.

103. U.S. Department of Homeland Security National Preparedness Task Force, *Civil Defense and Homeland Security*, 12.

104. U.S. Department of Defense, Office of Civil Defense, *Family Shelter Designs* (Washington, D.C.: Government Printing Office, 1962), 2–29,

http://www.civildefensemuseum.com/docs/FamilyShelterDesigns.pdf (accessed April 10, 2018).

105. Lynn Kennemer, *Elk City: Rising from the Prairie* (Elk City, OK: Western Oklahoma Historical Society, 2007), 118; Brewer, "Missiles of Oklahoma," 268.

106. "Students Ready for Emergency," *Southwestern*, February 6, 1962.

107. "Elk Siren Alert System Outlined," *Elk City Daily News*, October 25, 1962.

108. "State Civil Defense Steps Up Activity in Face of New Crisis," *Elk City Daily News*, October 25, 1962.

109. "Defense Program Mapped: Alert System Test Due Tuesday," *Elk City Daily News*, October 26, 1962.

110. Ibid.

111. "Civil Defense Plan Reviewed," *Altus Times-Democrat*, October 23, 1962.

112. "Courses Planned in Civil Defense," *Southwestern*, October 30, 1962.

113. "Classes at Canute: Area Survival Course Will Start on Monday," *Elk City Daily News*, November 4, 1962.

114. Kennemer, *Elk City*, 118.

115. "Community Fallout Shelter Supplies—Water Storage Drums," Civil Defense Museum, accessed April 12, 2018, http://www.civildefensemuseum.com/cdmuseum2/supply/water.html.

116. U.S. Department of Defense, Office of Civil Defense, *Federal Civil Defense Guide*, Part D, Chapter 2, Appendix 6, "Fallout Shelter Food Requirements" (Washington, D.C.: Government Printing Office, 1964), 1–2, http://www.civildefensemuseum.com/docs/fcdg/FCDG%20Pt%20D%20Ch%20 2%20App%206.pdf (accessed April 12, 2018).

117. U.S. Department of Defense, Office of Civil Defense, *Federal Civil Defense Guide*, Part D, Chapter 2, Appendix 8, "Fallout Shelter Medical Kit" (Washington, D.C.: Government Printing Office, 1964), 1–2, http://www.civildefensemuseum.com/docs/fcdg/FCDG%20Pt%20D%20 Ch%202%20App%208.pdf (accessed April 12, 2018).

118. Wertz, "From Nuclear Fallout to Tornadoes," StateImpact Oklahoma; "Provisions Arrive to Stock Shelters," *Southwestern*, October 13, 1964.

119. "Civil-Defense Minded Professor Digging Storm and Fallout Shelter— 'For Exercise,' " *Southwestern*, December 8, 1964.

120. Ibid.

121. Basil Weatherly, interview by the author, June 30, 2018.

122. Ibid.

123. Ibid.

124. Ibid.

125. Ibid.

126. Ibid.

127. Ibid.

128. Blanchard, *American Civil Defense 1945–1984*, 11–12, 14–15; U.S. Department of Homeland Security National Preparedness Task Force, *Civil Defense and Homeland Security*, 13–14.

129. Bob Klaassen, interview by the author via email, May 13, 2018.

130. "Federal Sirens," Civil Defense Museum, accessed July 4, 2018, http://www.civildefensemuseum.com/sirens/sirenpx2.html.

131. Billy Word, interview by the author, May 16, 2018.

Chapter 7

132. Tony Williams, "Crisis Relocation Plan Mushrooms as Nuclear Concern Grows," *Daily Oklahoman*, June 6, 1982, accessed April 12, 2018, https://newsok.com/article/1986045/crisis-relocation-plan-mushrooms-as-nuclear-concern-grows.

133. Ibid.

134. Ibid.

135. Michael Crowden, "City Has Nuclear War Plan," *Daily Oklahoman*, April 7, 1982, accessed April 12, 2018, https://newsok.com/article/1979479/city-has-nuclear-war-plan.

136. Ibid.

137. Ellie Sutter, "Council Must Decide How Stale Crackers Crumble," *Daily Oklahoman*, July 27, 1988, accessed April 12, 2018, https://newsok.com/article/2233642/council-must-decide-how-stale-crackers-crumble.

Chapter 8

138. "Tinker Air Force Base Fact Sheet," Tinker Air Force Base, accessed July 16, 2018, http://www.tinker.af.mil/About-Us/Fact-Sheets/Display/Article/384766/tinker-air-force-base-fact-sheet/.

139. James L. Crowder, "Tinker Air Force Base," *Encyclopedia of Oklahoma History and Culture*, accessed July 16, 2018, https://www.okhistory.org/publications/enc/entry.php?entry=TI004.

140. Ibid.

141. Greg L. Davis, "Tinker History: Boeing KC-135 Stratotanker," Tinker Air Force Base, June 26, 2017, accessed July 16, 2018, http://www.tinker.af.mil/DesktopModules/ArticleCS/Print.aspx?PortalId=106&ModuleId=14616&Article=1229539.

142. Paul Monies, "Tinker, Boeing Share Long History," *NewsOK*, October 22, 2017, accessed July 16, 2018, https://newsok.com/article/5566060/tinker-boeing-share-long-history.

143. Adam Kemp, "Oklahomans at Tinker Air Force Base Make Sure B-52s Keep Soaring," *NewsOK*, January 26, 2014, accessed July 16, 2018, https://newsok.com/article/3924058/oklahomans-at-tinker-air-force-base-make-sure-b-52s-keep-soaring.

144. Greg L. Davis, "Tinker History: Boeing AGM-28 'Hound Dog' Missile," *Journal Record*, May 16, 2017, accessed July 16, 2018, http://journalrecord.com/tinkertakeoff/2017/05/16/tinker-history-boeing-agm-28-hound-dog-missile/.

145. Thomas L. Hedglen, "Vance Air Force Base," *Encyclopedia of Oklahoma History and Culture*, accessed July 16, 2018, https://www.okhistory.org/publications/enc/entry.php?entry=VA005.

146. Jeff Mullin, "A Legacy of Flight: Vance AFB Celebrates 75 Years," *Enid News & Eagle*, November 21, 2016, accessed July 16, 2018, https://www.enidnews.com/news/a-legacy-of-flight-vance-afb-celebrates-years/article_2a840994-b007-11e6-8250-93242942ed93.html.

147. Hedglen, "Vance Air Force Base," *Encyclopedia of Oklahoma History and Culture*.

148. James L. Crowder, "Clinton-Sherman Air Force Base," *Encyclopedia of Oklahoma History and Culture*, accessed July 16, 2018, https://www.okhistory.org/publications/enc/entry.php?entry=CL017.

149. Ibid.

150. Ibid.

151. Ron Jackson, "Burns Flat and Surroundings Surprised by Air Base Closure," *NewsOK*, February 13, 2005, accessed July 16, 2018, https://newsok.com/article/1419130/burns-flat-and-surroundings-surprised-by-air-base-closure.

152. Ibid.

153. Ibid.

154. Matthew Rex Cox, "U.S. Naval Ammunition Depot," *Encyclopedia of Oklahoma History and Culture*, accessed July 21, 2018, https://www.okhistory.org/publications/enc/entry.php?entry=US002.

155. Ibid.

156. Lance Janda, "Fort Sill," *Encyclopedia of Oklahoma History and Culture*, accessed July 17, 2018, https://www.okhistory.org/publications/enc/entry.php?entry=FO038.

157. Ibid.

158. "Wars: The Cold War," Fort Sill, accessed July 17, 2018, http://sill-www.army.mil/History/_wars/coldwar.htm.

159. Janda, "Fort Sill," *Encyclopedia of Oklahoma History and Culture*.

160. "Atomic Cannon," RoadsideAmerica.com, accessed July 17, 2018, https://www.roadsideamerica.com/story/11525.

161. "Wars: The Cold War," Fort Sill.

162. Richard S. Guinan, "Altus Air Force Base," *Encyclopedia of Oklahoma History and Culture*, accessed July 17, 2018, https://www.okhistory.org/publications/enc/entry.php?entry=AL014.

163. Ibid.

Chapter 9

164. Erin M. Sloan, "Albert, Carl Bert," *Encyclopedia of Oklahoma History and Culture*, accessed July 17, 2018, https://www.okhistory.org/publications/enc/entry.php?entry=AL003; "Carl Bert Albert, a Powerful Democrat in Congress for Three Decades, Is Dead at 91," *New York Times*, February 6, 2000, accessed July 17, 2018, https://www.nytimes.com/2000/02/06/us/carl-bert-albert-a-powerful-democrat-in-congress-for-three-decades-is-dead-at-91.html.

165. Sloan, "Albert, Carl Bert," *Encyclopedia of Oklahoma History and Culture*; "Carl Bert Albert, a Powerful Democrat in Congress for Three Decades, Is Dead at 91," *New York Times*.

166. "Carl Bert Albert, a Powerful Democrat in Congress for Three Decades, Is Dead at 91," *New York Times*.

167. Sloan, "Albert, Carl Bert," *Encyclopedia of Oklahoma History and Culture*; "Carl Bert Albert, a Powerful Democrat in Congress for Three Decades, Is Dead at 91," *New York Times*.

168. Sloan, "Albert, Carl Bert," *Encyclopedia of Oklahoma History and Culture*.

169. "Carl Bert Albert, a Powerful Democrat in Congress for Three Decades, Is Dead at 91," *New York Times*.

170. Sloan, "Albert, Carl Bert," *Encyclopedia of Oklahoma History and Culture*; "Carl Bert Albert, a Powerful Democrat in Congress for Three Decades, Is Dead at 91," *New York Times*.

171. "Carl Bert Albert, a Powerful Democrat in Congress for Three Decades, Is Dead at 91," *New York Times*.

172. Carl Albert and Danney Goble, *Little Giant: The Life and Times of Speaker Carl Albert* (Norman: University of Oklahoma Press, 1990), 264.

173. Ibid., 264–65.

174. "Carl Albert Center," University of Oklahoma, accessed July 17, 2018, http://www.ou.edu/carlalbertcenter.

175. "Carl Bert Albert, a Powerful Democrat in Congress for Three Decades, Is Dead at 91," *New York Times*.

176. "Biographical Data: Thomas P. Stafford, Lieutenant General, USAF (Ret.) NASA Astronaut (Former)," NASA, accessed July 18, 2018, https://www.jsc.nasa.gov/Bios/htmlbios/stafford-tp.html; "Lieutenant General Thomas P. Stafford," U.S. Air Force, accessed July 18, 2018, http://www.af.mil/About-Us/Biographies/Display/Article/105575/lieutenant-general-thomas-p-stafford/.

177. "Biographical Data: Thomas P. Stafford, Lieutenant General, USAF (Ret.) NASA Astronaut (Former)," NASA, accessed July 18, 2018, https://www.jsc.nasa.gov/Bios/htmlbios/stafford-tp.html.

178. Robert Dallek, *An Unfinished Life: John Kennedy, 1917–1963* (Boston: Little, Brown, 2003), 651.

179. "Astronauts: Thomas Stafford," Astronaut Scholarship Foundation, accessed July 18, 2018, https://www.astronautscholarship.org/Astronauts/thomas-p-stafford/.

180. "Biographical Data: Thomas P. Stafford, Lieutenant General, USAF (Ret.) NASA Astronaut (Former)," NASA, accessed July 18, 2018, https://www.jsc.nasa.gov/Bios/htmlbios/stafford-tp.html.

181. "Astronauts: Thomas Stafford," Astronaut Scholarship Foundation, accessed July 18, 2018, https://www.astronautscholarship.org/Astronauts/thomas-p-stafford/.

182. "Biographical Data: Thomas P. Stafford, Lieutenant General, USAF (Ret.) NASA Astronaut (Former)," NASA, accessed July 18, 2018, https://www.jsc.nasa.gov/Bios/htmlbios/stafford-tp.html.

183. Ibid.

184. Ibid.

185. "Gen. Thomas P. Stafford Center (STF)," Southwestern Oklahoma State University, accessed July 19, 2018, http://myatlascms.com/map/?id=768#!s/key=stafford%20center?m/96426.

186. Stafford Air & Space Museum, accessed July 19, 2018, https://staffordmuseum.org/.

Chatper 10

187. Don S. Kirschner, *Cold War Exile: The Unclosed Case of Maurice Halperin* (Columbia: University of Missouri Press, 1995), 17, 19–21.

188. Ibid., 23–24, 32.

189. Ibid., 34, 36.

190. Ibid., 36–37.

191. Ibid., 39.

192. Ibid., 39–40.

193. Ibid., 41–42.

194. Ibid., 49–55.

195. Ibid., 56.

196. Ibid., 57.

197. Ibid., 58.

198. George Lynn Cross, *Professors, Presidents & Politicians: Civil Rights and the University of Oklahoma, 1890–1968* (Norman: University of Oklahoma Press, 1981), 112; Eric Eugene Beau, "Leon Phillips and the New Deal in Oklahoma" (master's thesis, University of Central Oklahoma, 2015), 46–47, 49.

199. Beau, "Leon Phillips and the New Deal," 52–53.

200. Ibid., 61–62.

201. Ibid., 64–65; Wayne A. Wiegand and Shirley A. Wiegand, "Sooner State Civil Liberties in Perilous Times, 1940–1941, Part 2: Oklahoma's Little Dies Committee," *Chronicles of Oklahoma* 85 (Spring 2007): 7.

202. Beau, "Leon Phillips and the New Deal," 66.

203. Cross, *Professors, Presidents & Politicians*, 124.

204. Kirschner, *Cold War Exile*, 60–61; Wiegand and Wiegand, "Sooner State Civil Liberties," 23, 25.

205. Beau, "Leon Phillips and the New Deal," 69.

206. Ibid., 70–71.

207. Kirschner, *Cold War Exile*, 112–16.

208. Kati Marton, *True Believer: Stalin's Last American Spy* (New York: Simon & Schuster, 2016), 50, 72.

209. Ibid., 114.

210. Ibid., 42–43, 50.

211. Kirschner, *Cold War Exile*, 118, 127–29.

212. Ibid., 130–31.

213. Ibid., 133.

214. Ibid., 134–35, 137–40.

215. Ibid., 277.

216. Ibid.

217. Ibid., 278–79.

218. Ibid., 279–80.

219. Ibid., 280–81.

220. Ibid., 281–82, 302.

221. Ibid., 282.

222. Ibid., 290–92.

223. Ibid., 314.

224. Ibid., 315–16.

225. John Earl Haynes and Harvey Klehr, *Venona: Decoding Soviet Espionage in America* (New Haven: Yale University Press, 1999), 6, 8–10.

226. Ibid., 101–2

227. Ibid.

228. Ibid., 102–3.

229. Allen Weinstein and Alexander Vassiliev, *The Haunted Wood: Soviet Espionage in America—The Stalin Era* (New York: Random House, 1999), xxiii, 106, 256.

230. Haynes and Klehr, *Venona*, 9–11, 15–16, 35–36, 90, 129–30, 160–61, 163, 170–73, 220, 223–24, 307–11, 331–32.

Chapter 11

231. Ibid., 22.

232. Marton, *True Believer*, 44, 50.

233. Haynes and Klehr, *Venona*, 22.

Chapter 12

234. Scott D. Hughes, "Cold War," *Encyclopedia of the Great Plains*, University of Nebraska Lincoln, accessed July 23, 2018, http://plainshumanities.unl.edu/encyclopedia/doc/egp.war.012.

235. Ibid.

236. "U.S. Military Fatal Casualties of the Korean War for Home-State-of-Record: Oklahoma," National Archives, accessed July 24, 2018, https://www.archives.gov/files/research/military/korean-war/casualty-lists/ok-alpha.pdf.

237. "U.S. Military Fatal Casualties of the Vietnam War for Home-State-of-Record: Oklahoma," National Archives, accessed July 24, 2018, https://www.archives.gov/files/research/military/vietnam-war/casualty-lists/ok-alpha.pdf.

238. Hughes, "Cold War," *Encyclopedia of the Great Plains*.

239. Colleen Kane, "7 Doomsday Bunkers for Surviving the Apocalypse, No Matter Your Budget," *Money*, February 10, 2017, accessed July 24, 2018, http://time.com/money/4665985/doomsday-bunkers-survive-apocalypse-sale/.

240. Hughes, "Cold War," *Encyclopedia of the Great Plains*.

241. Clark Clifford and Richard Holbrooke, *Counsel to the President: A Memoir* (New York: Random House, 1991), 660.

INDEX

ABOUT THE AUTHOR

Landry Brewer is Bernhardt Instructor of History for Southwestern Oklahoma State University and teaches at the Sayre campus.

Though he has been published multiple times in the journal of the Oklahoma Historical Society, several times in Oklahoma newspapers and has written two one-act plays that have been performed, this is Brewer's first book.

He and his wife, Erin, have five children and live in Elk City.